The Protestant Church and the Negro

The Protestant Church *and the* Negro

A PATTERN OF SEGREGATION

by Frank S. Loescher

With a Foreword by
Bishop William Scarlett

NEGRO UNIVERSITIES PRESS
WESTPORT, CONNECTICUT

Copyright 1948 by The International Committee of Young Men's Christian Associations

Originally published in 1948
by Association Press, New York

Reprinted with the permission
of Association Press

Reprinted in 1971 by Negro Universities Press
Division of Greenwood Press, Inc.
Westport, Connecticut

Library of Congress Catalogue Card Number 76-135601

ISBN 0-8371-5193-7

Printed in the United States of America

To My Wife

Contents

The problem. Growing awareness of the problem. Seventeen denominations examined. How the evidence was obtained. Toward racial integration. Deep are the roots. Summary.

Before the depression. During the depression. World War II. Jim Crow in the Church. Since the war. Shortcomings. How effective are pronouncements? Summary.

Denominations with Negro churches. Denominations which segregate. Denominations which integrate. The Methodist arrangement. What happens at conventions. The Methodist compromise. Wanted: more knowledge. Summary.

Foreword

THIS BOOK will be unpleasant reading for those who love the Church.

The author is himself a Protestant, a member of the Society of Friends. For six years he taught in an Episcopal boys' preparatory school, and for six years he was a professor of sociology in a Methodist college. He is now a secretary for race relations of the American Friends Service Committee, and lecturer in sociology at Temple University. In 1944 he was selected as research worker for the Federal Council of Churches' Commission on the Church and Minority Peoples. The present manuscript, however, is entirely separate from his report to the Federal Council. And for the opinions and conclusions which he reaches in this book neither the Federal Council nor its Commission on Minority Peoples has any responsibility.

Whether or not one agrees with the conclusions which the author draws from the facts set down in this book, the facts themselves must be faced. They are bitter facts. Though there have been many notable exceptions, the Church has acquiesced in the pattern of segregation. And the reading of this book leaves one with a very uneasy conscience and gives rise to searching self-examination and self-accusation.

For on purely religious grounds there is no defense for segregation within the Church. In the presence of God the divisions of race are transcended: "There is neither Greek nor Jew, Barbarian, Scythian, bond nor free; but

9

Christ is all, and in all." All men are God's children; all are within the circle of his equal concern. "Have we not all one Father? Hath not one God created us?" This principle segregation denies. For segregation is not only a barrier to the elemental equality of opportunity which we in this Democracy so generally profess as our necessary goal. It is more sweeping than that. It is, in itself, an implication of inferiority, an inferiority not only of status but of essence, of being. Therefore, it offends profoundly against the religious principle.

The tide has set in against segregation within the Church. The action taken by the special session of the Federal Council of Churches held in Columbus in the spring of 1946, renouncing the "pattern of segregation in race relations as unnecessary and undesirable, and a violation of the gospel of love and human brotherhood," and calling on its constituent communions to go and do likewise, is an indication of what is happening in many minds and will come to life in many places. This tide will gather momentum. And the reading of this book will accelerate this movement. The Protestant Church is not an authoritarian organization. It proceeds by the democratic process, which means that leadership must carry the people with it. The process may be somewhat slow. But there has been ample opportunity for the education of our people; the time for action is now at hand.

There is a tendency to underestimate the number of people willing to follow persuasive Christian leadership, as there is also a tendency to overestimate the repercussions which will follow decisive Christian action. Repercussions there will be. The important thing, however, is not whether our churches are larger or smaller. The essential point is that those within the Church be committed to the Christian Cause.

WILLIAM SCARLETT, *Diocese of Missouri*
St. Louis, 1948

Acknowledgments

It is a pleasure to acknowledge my appreciation to the many persons who have helped to make possible this investigation: Bradford S. Abernethy, director, and Will W. Alexander, chairman, of the Commission on the Church and Minority Peoples of the Federal Council of Churches, under whose authorization I collected the facts on policies and practices; Charles S. Johnson and his associates of the Race Relations Division of the American Missionary Association, Fisk University, where in 1944 I began this study; and the thousands of other persons who made available the facts of racial practice in churches and schools.

Ray H. Abrams of the University of Pennsylvania, Dwight L. Culver of Purdue University, Charles R. Lawrence, Jr., formerly of Fisk University, J. Oscar Lee of the Federal Council of Churches, and Arthur L. Swift, Jr., of Union Theological Seminary have read this manuscript and given me the benefit of their knowledge. The Right Reverend William Scarlett, besides writing the Foreword, has made several valuable criticisms. Warren D. Smith of Rhode Island State University aided in methods of expression. None of the persons named above is responsible for the interpretations and conclusions.

The editors and publishers of the journals listed below have kindly permitted me to reproduce some of the material which I originally published in the following articles: "Racial Policies and Practices of Major National Protestant Denominations," *Phylon*, Third Quarter, 1947; "The

Church and Interracial Reform," *Journal of Religion,*
October, 1947; "The Protestant Church and the Negro:
Recent Pronouncements," *Social Forces,* December, 1947;
"The Racial Practices of Protestant Colleges and Univer-
sities," *Journal of Higher Education,* to be published later.

I am grateful to the following publishers, agencies, peri-
odicals, and individuals for permission to quote: Abingdon-
Cokesbury Press, Council of Church Boards of Education,
Federal Council of Churches, Fisk University Press, Har-
per & Brothers, Harvard University Press, D. C. Heath &
Co., International Council of Religious Education, The
Josephite Press, Longmans, Green & Co., Simon & Schuster,
Inc., U. S. Office of Education, University of North Caro-
lina Press, Willett, Clark & Co., Yale University Press; also
to *American Journal of Sociology, The Christian Century,
Events and Trends in Race Relations, Friends Intelli-
gencer, Harper's Magazine, Journal of Negro Education,
Journal of Social Issues, New Yorker, Philadelphia Record,
Survey Graphic, World Almanac, 1945,* and *Zion's Herald;*
also to Howard McClain; also to Church of the Brethren,
Congregational Christian Churches, Disciples of Christ,
Evangelical Church, Evangelical and Reformed Church,
Friends General Conference, The Methodist Church,
Northern Baptist Convention, Presbyterian Church in the
U.S., Presbyterian Church in the U.S.A., Religious Society
of Friends (Five Years Meeting), Protestant Episcopal
Church, Reformed Church in America, Southern Baptist
Convention, United Brethren in Christ, United Lutheran
Church, United Presbyterian Church.

Throughout the study and writing my wife has been my
constant companion and partner.

Philadelphia, 1948   FRANK S. LOESCHER

List of Tables

CHAPTER 1

The Protestant Church and the Negro

PROTESTANTISM, by its policies and practices, far from helping to integrate the Negro in American life, is actually contributing to the segregation of Negro Americans.

Millions of sincere church members will be shocked by this statement. Some may challenge the truth of it. This book presents the evidence.

THE PROBLEM

The relationship between the Protestant Church and the Negro has been a neglected area of investigation. The racial policies and practices of organized labor, industry, government, public education, and the Army and Navy have been studied intensively. The effect of these institutions on the economic welfare of Negroes is an obvious reason for investigating segregation and discrimination in them. In comparison, the economic role of the church is relatively unimportant.

But the church, like every other social institution, provides a medium for human association. If a people lack social contacts in the major institutions of a society, they are isolated or segregated, while a people freely participating in the total life of a society are integrated. It is the integrating and segregating function of the church with which we are concerned.

Our thesis is that the Protestant church in general, by the practices of its congregations and educational institutions, is following the status quo in Negro-white relationships and that the Protestant Church as a social institution is not actively furthering the integration of the Negro into American society.

As evidence we shall show that by and large the churches in their pronouncements are just beginning to sense the social implications of the caste-like status of the American Negro people. Furthermore, the churches in their denominational policies avoid making public their position on crucial types of relationships with Negroes. Finally, and most telling of all, the churches in their congregations and educational institutions adhere to a pattern of segregation.

GROWING AWARENESS OF THE PROBLEM

There is some evidence that during the war the American Negro became a problem to the conscience of American Protestantism—a problem in the sense used by Gunnar Myrdal in *An American Dilemma*. The Negro, according to Myrdal, is a problem to most Americans because of the conflict between the American creed and the American deed.[1]

As far back as 1921 the Federal Council of the Churches of Christ in America had recognized the problem and had established a Department of Race Relations. This department for years tried to sensitize Protestants, but there was little denominational recognition of the heart of the problem—segregation.

In the past few years, however, some Protestant denominations have indicated by their pronouncements at national conventions that they are becoming more aware of the significance of the status of the Negro in American life and also of the necessity for applying the principles of Christianity and democracy to the Negro. Recently sever-

---

[1] Myrdal, Gunnar, *An American Dilemma* (New York: Harper & Brothers, 1944) , I, xliii.

al denominations have recommended that racial fellowship be practiced in the local church.

In 1942 the Federal Council of Churches, representing twenty-five Protestant denominations with over twenty-five million members, appointed a special commission "in the light of two urgent needs:

1. to strengthen the bases of democracy at home,
2. to make more effective the Church's witness to and practice of the Christian principle of brotherhood."[2]

This body, the Commission on the Church and Minority Peoples, planned a national study conference and undertook to secure material on denominational principles, policies, and practices on the relationship of the church to minority peoples in four areas: church membership, ecclesiastical structure, educational institutions, and denominational conventions.[3]

Summaries of material obtained in this study were used in an official statement, *The Church and Race Relations,* approved by a special meeting of The Federal Council of the Churches of Christ in America in March, 1946. The Federal Council renounced "the pattern of segregation as unnecessary and undesirable and a violation of the gospel of love and human brotherhood," requested its "constituent communions to do likewise," and called upon them to work for "a non-segregated Church and a non-segregated

---

[2] "Commission on the Church and Minority Peoples," instituted by The Federal Council of the Churches of Christ in America, p. 2. (Leaflet.)

[3] Missionary policies have been studied by Wilbur C. Harr and Bodine Tenney Porter. See Harr, Wilbur C., *The Negro as an American Protestant Missionary in Africa,* unpublished Ph.D. dissertation, Divinity School, University of Chicago, 1945; also Porter, Bodine Tenney, *What are the Policies, Practices, and Attitudes of the Foreign Mission Boards in North America with Reference to the Sending of American Negroes as Foreign Missionaries?* M.A. thesis, Presbyterian College of Christian Education, 1945, mimeographed by the Foreign Missions Conference of North America, New York, 1945.

society."[4] Here is evidence of a growing awareness of the problem at the national interdenominational level.

What can be said about other levels? Are all the constituent denominations of the Federal Council becoming equally sensitive to the problem? What are the practices of their congregations, schools, colleges, and seminaries?

Seventeen Denominations Examined

There are over two hundred separate Protestant denominations. Most of these are small bodies with no relationship to the Federal Council of Churches. Of the twenty-five denominations represented in the Federal Council of Churches of Christ in America, fifteen of the largest, predominantly white, were selected for study. (See the list on p. 19.) In this group of churches we have almost every Protestant denomination in the liberal movement of Christianity.

One might assume that if any churches practice the "social gospel" it would be these members of the Federal Council of Churches, a federation created in 1905 in order more fully to manifest "the essential oneness of the Christian Churches of America in Jesus Christ as their Divine Lord and Saviour, and to promote the spirit of fellowship, service and cooperation among them." Among other objects the Federal Council was

To bring the Christian bodies of America into united service for Christ and the world.

To secure a larger combined influence for the Churches of Christ in all matters affecting the moral and social condition of the people, so as to promote the application of the law of Christ in every relation of human life.[5]

---

[4] *The Church and Race Relations* (New York: Department of Race Relations, The Federal Council of the Churches of Christ in America, 1946), p. 5.

[5] "Inter-Church Conference on Federation," *Church Federation*, Elias B. Sanford, ed. (New York, 1906), pp. 33-34, cited by Hopkins, Charles How-

The fifteen largest "white" denominations in the Federal Council, with their 1943-44 inclusive memberships are (omitting the Russian Orthodox Church):[6]

1.	The Methodist Church	8,046,129
2.	Protestant Episcopal Church	2,227,524
3.	Presbyterian Church in the U.S.A.	2,040,399
4.	United Lutheran Church (consultative)	1,690,204
5.	Disciples of Christ	1,672,354
6.	Northern Baptist Convention	1,555,914
7.	Congregational Christian Churches	1,075,401
8.	Evangelical and Reformed Church	675,958
9.	Presbyterian Church in the U.S.	565,853
10.	United Brethren in Christ	433,480
11.	Evangelical Church	255,881
12.	United Presbyterian Church	193,637
13.	Church of the Brethren	180,287
14.	Reformed Church in America	169,390
15.	Religious Society of Friends (Five Years Meeting)	70,000

---

ard, in *The Rise of the Social Gospel in American Protestantism*, 1865-1915 (New Haven: Yale University Press, 1940) , p. 305.

[6] Landis, Benson Y., ed., *Yearbook of American Churches* (The Federal Council of the Churches of Christ in America, 1945), p. 89.

The following "Negro" denominations are omitted:

16.	National Baptist Convention, Inc.	4,021,618
17.	African Methodist Episcopal Church	868,735
18.	African Methodist Episcopal Zion Church	489,244
19.	Colored Methodist Episcopal Church	382,000

The following "white" denominations are omitted:

20.	Russian Orthodox Church	300,000
21.	Moravian Church	40,764
22.	Ukrainian Orthodox Church of America	39,500
23.	Syrian Antiochian Orthodox Church	20,300
24.	Seventh Day Baptist General Conference	6,581

The United Church of Canada (affiliated) is also omitted   728,814

Total Membership 27,749,967

In November, 1946, The Church of the United Brethren in Christ and The Evangelical Church were united and now constitute The Evangelical United Brethren Church. They are treated separately in this book.

Two branches of Protestantism that are not members of the Federal Council are also included in the study—the Southern Baptist Convention and the Friends General Conference. The Southern Baptists, with 5,667,926 members, are the largest denomination in the South and are exceeded in membership nationally only by the Methodists. Even though the Southern Baptists are, with a few exceptions, conservative theologically and socially, by sheer weight of numbers their potential influence in race relations is enormous. On the other hand, the Friends General Conference, an organization composed largely of eastern Yearly Meetings, has only 17,870 members. But, beginning in 1688, the testimony and practice of these Friends placed them for a century and a half in the forefront of the anti-slavery movement. While for these reasons the Southern Baptists and the eastern Quakers are included, the racial principles, policies, and practices of the member bodies in the Federal Council of Churches remain the major focus of interest in this report.

These fifteen bodies in the Federal Council, the Southern Baptists, and the Friends General Conference have an inclusive membership of approximately 25,000,000, about 80 per cent of the white Protestants in the United States.

No denominations that are predominantly Negro are included. As Liston Pope says:

When one looks at the Negro churches instead of the white, the prevalence of segregation is likewise apparent. There is one crucial difference: the Negro church is a segregated but not a *segregating* institution. About a decade ago, 800 Negro churches were asked whether they objected to having white worshippers in their congregations. Not one replied in the affirmative.[7]

---

[7] Pope, Liston, "Caste in the Church: I. The Protestant Experience," *Survey Graphic*, Vol. XXXVI, No. 1 (January, 1947) p. 60.

How the Evidence Was Obtained

The pronouncements or resolutions to which frequent reference is made are taken from the official minutes of denominational conventions. Statements of policies and practices were obtained by means of an extensive questionnaire to selected officers of the denominations with an accompanying letter from the director of the Commission on the Church and Minority Peoples. Other information was secured from interviews with denominational officers, from books and religious periodicals, and from some field observation.

After it was found that denominational headquarters did not have adequate information on Negro membership in predominantly white churches or Negro students in predominantly white schools, colleges, and seminaries, a survey by mail was made of approximately eighteen thousand churches in six denominations and several hundred church colleges, junior colleges, schools, and seminaries.

Since congregational membership is the crucial test of the principle of Christian brotherhood, it was believed a survey of Negro membership in these congregations would provide a convenient and practicable means of measuring the extent of segregation in Protestantism.

There are approximately 120,000 white Protestant churches in the seventeen denominations of our study. Protestantism, however, can affect the integration of Negroes through other channels. Outside the southern system of segregated education there are several hundred educational institutions controlled by these same Protestant denominations. The admission and employment practices of these educational agencies offer additional indexes of the role of Protestantism in the integration of Negro Americans.

In order to trace the pattern of segregation in the churches, considerable data have been assembled also on ecclesiastical structure and denominational conventions and assemblies, but church membership and educational enrollment are the chief bases used for measuring practice.

TOWARD RACIAL INTEGRATION

What is integration? Buell G. Gallagher cogently states the position of the integrationist:

... The integrationist position is precisely what the Christian ethic requires—that every man, woman, and child shall be free to enter into, and to contribute to, the welfare of all mankind, without any restrictions or disabilities based on color caste— and without any advantages because of color or the lack of it.[8]

Many people, however, believe that cultural differences make integration impossible. But the integrationist believes that these differences are greatly exaggerated. In religion, for example, almost all Negroes are Protestants and nine-tenths of all Negro church members are either Baptists or Methodists,[9] with forms of worship and church government like those of Baptists and Methodists everywhere.

Not only in religion is the Negro like the majority group in the United States. In other aspects of our culture as well his tastes are like those of his fellows, whether in baseball or music, comics or politics.

In the past, his absorption of the "higher" aspects of our culture has been hindered by slavery, discrimination in education, employment, and political expression—and by segregation in schools, churches, jobs, and housing.

Weatherford and Johnson in the early thirties said:

The standards of living are different, it is true, but the difference is not cultural; one is simply higher in the scale than the other. And all Negro standards of living are not low. The

---

[8] Gallagher, Buell G., *Color and Conscience* (New York: Harper & Brothers, 1946) , p. 173.

[9] See Palmer, Edward Nelson, "The Religious Acculturation of the Negro," *Phylon,* Vol. V, No. 3, Third Quarter, 1944, pp. 260-265.

division is purely statistical. The code of morals by which Negroes live, however imperfectly, is European; the system of marriage is monogamy; the standards of justice and the law are American; vested property rights, the machine pattern of culture, are all Euro-American. Any American Negro who tried to live otherwise than by these codes and standards would quickly be crushed for his non-conformity. These are the basic elements of a culture, and conformity is the test of survival. There is not a Negro test of character, of capacity for self-maintenance, of intelligence, of law observance, of manners, of taste, or of aesthetic sense, that is not based upon this culture. When there is racial segregation it is not in terms of two cultures, but in terms of different planes of the same culture. The fact that there is discrimination is another way of indicating the identity of the cultures, for the term has no meaning when they are different. There is a strong suggestion that what is really meant is that these different planes should constitute the separate cultures.[10]

Today the differences are narrowing as Negroes move into the mainstream of American life.

These differences have played a part in the white American's refusal to accept Negro Americans socially. But they can be and have been greatly overemphasized as factors in the "problem." There are thousands of Negroes who from the standpoint of family background, educational attainment, professional achievement, and personality traits have mastered the "finest" products of western culture to a degree unequalled by millions of whites and yet they are still socially unacceptable to the whites.

To make clear what we mean by integration, consider the Protestant church in a preview of what is presented more fully in Chapters III and IV. The relationships of Negro Protestants to white Protestants fall into four possible patterns:

---

[10] Weatherford, Willis D. and Johnson, Charles S., *Race Relations*, (New York: D. C. Heath and Company, 1934) , p. 547.

First, there are Negroes who belong to Negro Protestant churches who never have any religious contact with white Protestants, for example, Colored Primitive Baptists. Not even the ministers or denominational leaders meet with white churchmen.

Second, there are the great separate Negro denominations—the National Baptist Convention, Inc., the African Methodist Episcopal Church, the African Methodist Episcopal Zion Church, the Colored Methodist Episcopal Church. There is no association between the members of these churches and their white brothers except for the contacts of denominational leaders in interdenominational bodies, such as The Federal Council of Churches or city councils of churches. A few hundred of these Negro Baptist churches, it is true, do belong to state conventions of the Northern Baptist Convention, but otherwise the five and one-half million members of these four large Negro denominations have no contacts with white churchmen.

In the third type, a somewhat closer relationship obtains among Negro and white members of predominantly white denominations, for instance, among the Presbyterians, Episcopalians, Congregationalists, and some others. Although well over 90 per cent of these Negro churchmen are in separate churches, these churches have representation in the local, regional, and national denominational organizations, and, therefore, a limited association with their white denominational brothers.

A fourth type of relationship is seen in those churches of predominantly white denominations which have a mixed membership. Here we sometimes have a relatively high degree of integration. Thus, there are some "white" churches which have Negro Sunday School superintendents, Negro members in the women's society, and Negro members on the board of control.[11]

DEEP ARE THE ROOTS

Many sociologists, when discussing the race problem in the United States, have said that the solution would require *amalgamation*.[12] And they usually have agreed that amalgamation is a matter of centuries. Integration, on the other hand, does not require amalgamation. However, it does require, among other things, that white churchmen forego their monopoly of economic power and admit Negroes to occupations and offices, within and without the church, from which they have been hitherto excluded. And to be successful, integration is dependent upon the breakdown of residential segregation.

Amalgamation is not the main problem or the immediate problem. The present need is for integration, for the abolition of segregation with its stamp of inferiority and inferior opportunities for Negroes. A policy of integration can help to remove such stigma and disabilities. Integration in the church can advance the Negro's integration in the total society.

Integration will be more difficult to achieve than most churchmen realize, and for reasons which many probably do not suspect. While it is true that the so-called "Negro problem" is in reality a white man's problem, many Negroes will probably be as reluctant to unite with white churches as white churchmen will be to extend a welcome. The evidence is almost conclusive that many Negroes not

---

[11] The Interracial Church and the Interracial Religious Fellowship might be considered a fifth type. Such groups now exist in Philadelphia, New York, Washington and other cities. See Homer A. Jack, "The Emergence of the Interracial Church," *Social Action*, Vol. XIII, No. 1 (January, 1947), pp. 31-38. These interracial and interfaith organizations have been established in recent years by people unable to find a satisfying fellowship in their own churches. In general, they are outside of the denominational structure.

[12] For example, Reuter, Edward Byron, *The American Race Problem* (Revised Edition, New York: Thomas Y. Crowell Company, 1938), pp. 410-419.

only do not desire association with whites but that they will be suspicious for a long time of any offers of welcome by the church or its educational institutions. This applies also to Negro preachers, says Myrdal, who points to their vested interest in segregated churches. They feel, often with some justification, that interracial religious activity would mean having white men as church leaders for Negroes but not Negroes as church leaders for whites.[13]

As compensation for the position of inferiority in which they are held by whites, there has developed both in the North and in the South a race consciousness and race pride which permeate all classes of Negroes, but especially the Negro middle and upper class. Consider these passages from Myrdal's chapter on the "Effects of Social Inequality":

. . . These middle and upper class Negroes, who have stepped out of the servant status, live mostly by catering to their own people. Not only have their economic contacts with whites been reduced but, because they know they are not liked by whites and are likely to feel humiliated in all contacts with them, they avoid whites in all other spheres of life. . . .

. . . Measured in terms of the number of personal contacts with white people, there are Negro doctors, dentists, teachers, preachers, morticians, and druggists in the South who might as well be living in a foreign country. . . .

Mutual ignorance and the paucity of common interests is a barrier to, and a modifier of, social contact between even educated and liberal whites and Negroes in the North, even in the extraordinary circles where segregation and discrimination play no role. . . . The Negro is an alien in America, and in a sense this becomes the more evident when he steps out of his old role

---

[13] Myrdal, Gunnar, *op. cit.*, II, p. 870. However, one hundred prominent Negro churchmen have recently asked for the abolition of race segregation in the Church. See *Negro Churchmen Speak to White Churchmen*, published by the Commission on the Church and Minority Peoples, The Federal Council of the Churches of Christ in America, New York, 1944. Also see Nelson, William Stuart, ed., *The Christian Way in Race Relations* (Harper and Brothers, 1948).

of the servant who lives entirely for the comfort of his white superiors. Ignorance and disparity of interests, arising out of segregation and discrimination on the part of whites, increased by voluntary withdrawal and race pride on the part of Negroes, becomes itself an important element increasing and perpetuating isolation between the groups.[14]

SUMMARY

Relationships between white and Negro people present a dilemma of increasingly serious importance in American life. Protestantism is deeply involved in this problem. It cannot escape responsibility in relation to its solution, a responsibility of which it is becoming aware but in the discharge of which it has made only dim beginnings. The record of its policies and practices makes it evident that in many respects it has contributed to the seriousness of the very problem it should be helping to solve.

---

[14] Myrdal, Gunnar, *op. cit.*, I, pp. 645, 659.

CHAPTER 2

What the Churches Say

WHAT DO the Protestant churches say about race relations? How do they analyze the racial situation? Do the denominations favor fair employment practices legislation or oppose residential segregation through restrictive covenants by property owners?

Do any pronouncements call to the attention of their members the churches' own practices? Do any denominations issue pronouncements calling for fellowship in the local church? Do they evidence an interest in the racial policies of their schools, their colleges, their seminaries?

BEFORE THE DEPRESSION

Preceding 1929, very few pronouncements on race relations were made. F. Ernest Johnson in his book, *The Social Work of the Churches,* records only six in the period 1908-1929, most of which were adopted after World War I.[1]

---

[1] See Johnson, F. Ernest, ed., *The Social Work of the Churches* (New York: Department of Research and Education of the Federal Council of the Churches of Christ in America, 1930), pp. 154-155. These six statements are included in Appendix I, A. In addition to the six official denominational statements, many pronouncements were issued by the Federal Council of Churches and other *interdenominational* agencies. For example, in 1919 the Federal Council urged "equal economic . . . opportunities . . . parks . . . adequate schools, equal facilities . . . when traveling, adequate housing . . . police protection," and condemned lynching. *Ibid.*, p. 154. While our chief interest is in the denominations themselves, we do note the major pronouncements of the Federal Council in the text and cite them in the Appendix. With rare exceptions the denominational pronouncements lag behind the Federal Council's. This is shown in the 1919 statement on equal opportunity, quoted above, and in the 1924 pronouncement: "The assumption of inherent racial superiority by dominant groups around the world is neither supported by science nor justified by ethics."

Mob violence was the chief concern. Not untypical was the statement from the General Convention of the Protestant Episcopal Church:

Mob violence in every form is wrong; it is a clearly defined and imperative Christian duty to sustain the civil authorities in the righteous exercise of their powers in seeing that even-handed justice is unfailingly administered according to due and lawful processes.[2]

These few evidences of concern for the situation faced by the Negro are apparently the sum total of official denominational interest.[3] When one recalls the wave of race riots that swept the country after World War I, it is quite remarkable that so little concern was expressed. This era was marked by other trying situations for the Negro: his segregation in the army and navy, which brought strong protests from articulate Negroes; lynchings; the terrorizing of millions of Negroes by the Ku Klux Klan during its rebirth in the twenties; loss of employment in the postwar depression; discrimination by industry and unions; gross inequalities in housing, education, and medical care.

The churches were remarkably slow to speak out in defense of this helpless minority or to urge governmental action. Only one denomination, the Northern Baptists, called for action, and that only against lynching.[4]

Ibid., p. 155. Denominational statements comparable to these began to appear in the 1930's.

[2] *Ibid.*, p. 155.

[3] The denominations continued to contribute money for missionary work and benevolent enterprises, such as schools, colleges, and seminaries. "The record of the 'free' churches during the early decades of emancipation is the finest in American church history. A single board, the American Missionary Association of the Congregational Churches, started and supported 300 schools and colleges all over the South. Methodists, Baptists, Presbyterians, Episcopalians vied with one another in rushing education and the gospel to the freedmen," Embree, Edwin R., in Sperry, Willard, L., ed., *Religion and Our Racial Tensions* (Cambridge: Harvard University Press, 1945) , pp. 43-44. For a more detailed account of the churches' contribution to Negro education, see Embree, Edwin R., *Brown Americans* (New York: The Viking Press, 1943) , pp. 72-87.

Since religious groups adopted during this time resolutions on a variety of problems—child labor, collective bargaining, distribution of wealth, civil liberties, housing and health, the co-operative movement, international relations—there is considerable justification for observing that by the silence of most of its bodies Protestantism gave the appearance of having consented to what was happening to Negroes.

The common characteristic of all six statements of the seventeen denominations is that they deal with only the gross aspects of the treatment of Negroes, and then in the most general terms. The Congregationalists do use the term discrimination, but even they put the idea in a sentence that concludes with "there should be substituted full brotherly treatment for all races,"[5] which is as glittering a generality as that of the Methodist Episcopal, South: "Christ's teachings concerning human brotherhood demand equal justice and opportunity for all persons regardless of race, color or sex."[6]

DURING THE DEPRESSION

During the thirties over six hundred pronouncements on all kinds of social problems were made by the denominations and organizations affiliated with the International Council on Religious Education. Such social problems as alcohol and the liquor traffic, international relations, gambling, methods of social change, motion pictures, the agricultural situation, and race relations were among the chief objects of interest to the churches and church-related groups. Forty different statements on race relations were adopted, of which twenty-seven were endorsed by one or

---

4 Johnson, F. Ernest, ed. *op. cit.,* p. 155.

5 *Idem.*

6 *Idem.*

more denominations now associated with the Federal Council of Churches.[7]

Instead of six statements in a twenty-year period we now have twenty-seven with sixty endorsements in a single decade; indeed, the great majority of these resolutions came in the latter half of the thirties. The thirties might be called a "social problems decade"; the title of a book published in that period well describes the times—*Insurgent America.*[8]

The Negro, traditionally "the first to be fired and the last to be hired," was also insurgent. The Negro was beginning to count politically. As the spotlight was thrown on America's "ill-fed, ill-clothed, and ill-housed," Negroes were found to be experiencing far more than their proportionate share of these burdens. America began to awaken to what was happening to "every tenth man."

And yet the denominational pronouncements are quite general, still dealing for the most part only with the gross aspects of the disabilities and injustices experienced by Negroes. The majority of the statements focus on the most obvious evil—lynching—and scarcely a word is uttered on the more controversial and more basic issue of economic discrimination. Indeed, discrimination is rarely mentioned. And there is only a single use of the word segregation.

Eight Federal Council denominations and the Southern Baptists[9] protested in some fashion against lynching, five

---

[7] *Social Pronouncements,* 1930-1939 (Chicago: The International Council of Religious Education, n.d.), pp. 15-17. Note that in our discussion the quotations refer to the pronouncements in *Social Pronouncements.* In many cases the statements were abbreviated. The statements of the Southern Baptists have been listed separately, since they are not members of the International Council of Religious Education. See Appendix I, B.

Throughout our discussion of pronouncements we are concerned only with official denominational statements. Thus we do not include the report of the World Conference at Oxford.

[8] Bingham, Alfred M., *Insurgent America* (New York: Harper & Brothers, 1935).

members of the Federal Council endorsing bills before Congress. (See Appendix I B, page 123.) This is the only issue of a specific nature in the "terrible thirties" which commanded the support of most conventions.

On one other question action of a specific nature was taken, in this instance concerning a domestic problem of the churches with some Negro members. Three denominations resolved that "in making arrangements for conferences involving racial groups, care should be taken so that there will be no discrimination."[10] (See Appendix I B, page 123.)

The only other resolutions to receive general backing were the innocuous, "All races should enjoy same protection and rights" (seven bodies), and "Mutual good-will and cooperation among racial groups" (four churches).[11] (See Appendix I B, page 123.)

All of the other items were adopted by only one or, at the most, two denominations. These also deal in generalities and do not come to grips with basic factors, particularly the economic.

Two denominations, however, the Northern Baptists and the Congregational Christians, did say they were "opposed to all forced segregation."[12]

The Scottsboro case drew the attention of the Congregationalists and the Northern Presbyterians. Various resolutions urging efforts to change the attitudes of the church members were adopted by five denominations. The other resolutions, each adopted by one denomination, require little comment. Most significant, however, is the resolu-

---

[9] At eight conventions during the thirties the Southern Baptists condemned mob violence or lynching. In fact, until 1939—when they mentioned inequalities in the public schools, courts, wages, and employment opportunities—they took note of no other issue.

[10] *Social Pronouncements*, p. 15.

[11] *Idem.*

[12] *Idem.*

tion of the Northern Baptists who "condemn every discriminatory law, anti-racial organization, and all unfair tactics on part of labor or capital."[13] In many respects this statement epitomizes the attitude of most churches with respect to the Negro during the twentieth century—condemning discrimination in the law or industry or labor and failing to examine their own practices.

The pronouncements are as revealing for what they do not say as for what they do say. An examination of them quickly shows the extent to which the church was unaware of the shortcomings in its own practices. The Disciples did "urge approach to committee of National Convention of Negro Disciples to propose simultaneous conventions in same city at an early date,"[14] and they did "recommend to graduate schools of our brotherhood that action be initiated with opening of 1935-36 school year to offer equal opportunity for ministerial training for Negroes with white students in the ministry."[15] The Evangelical and Reformed Church said that they "favor inviting members of different races within our Church constituency to summer schools, camps, and local church meetings."[16] Since only three Japanese-American churches, one American Indian church, and no Negro churches are in the constituency, this was not as revolutionary as it might seem. We have already noted the statements on discrimination at conventions. Otherwise, these few resolutions reveal the limits of the churches' awareness of their own racial policies and practices.

---

[13] *Idem.*

[14] *Ibid.,* p. 16.

[15] *Idem.*

[16] *Ibid.,* p. 15. This pronouncement is one of the few instances of denominational statement being in advance of the Federal Council resolutions. In the thirties the Federal Council concentrated on removing discrimination from denominational conventions and lynching. See Appendix I B.

World War II

During the first five years of the present decade there has been no decline in denominational interest in race relations. This kind of witnessing for justice for the Negro really got going in the 1940's. The wave of pronouncements of the thirties appears to have become in the forties something of a flood. As previously noted, F. Ernest Johnson could find only six of them in the whole period from 1908 to 1929. In the next ten years there were twenty-seven, with sixty endorsements. But between 1940 and 1944, there were at least seventy-eight, with about ninety-three endorsements.[17] Consciences had been stirred, until some denominational leaders saw race as the number two problem of the churches, second only to world organization. A safer appraisal might be that in the minds of *certain denominational social-action secretaries* race is the number two problem. In any event, the churches, judged by their resolutions during World War II, are becoming more conscious of race. Even denominations which during the thirties had not made a single statement on race, for example, the United Presbyterian Church and the Evangelical Church, are now displaying an awareness of race tensions.

---

[17] The 1940-1944 social pronouncements of all denominations have not yet been brought together in printed form. See note in Appendix I C. Except where abbreviations are necessary to conserve space, the Appendix preserves the original wording.

The Southern Baptist resolutions are not included in these figures. Only pronouncements by the fifteen largest "white" denominations now affiliated with the Federal Council are counted in this summary. The number would be considerably increased by the addition of all of the Federal Council's own statements. For example, every February on Race Relations Sunday the Federal Council issues a lengthy statement which is widely used. All through the 1940's these Messages have very explicitly called attention to discrimination and segregation in churches, transportation, education, employment, and the armed services. These Messages can be secured from the Department of Race Relations, Federal Council of Churches, New York.

We have included in the text and Appendix the principal resolutions of the Federal Council.

Several matters are noteworthy in the most recent denominational pronouncements. In 1944, for the first time, economic discrimination was recognized in a forthright and specific manner: three denominations (Congregational Christian, Evangelical and Reformed, and Presbyterian U.S.A.) joined the Federal Council of Churches in endorsing the principles embodied in the work of the Fair Employment Practices Committee and favored Congressional action to set up a permanent FEPC. The Methodist Church also endorsed the principles of the FEPC, but did not come out in favor of legislative sanction. The Methodists ambiguously urged "all agencies involved in the administration of the act to improve the administration."[18]

On the poll tax issue no specific bill before Congress has been endorsed. The Presbyterians U.S.A. have stated that they are opposed to the disfranchisement of voters through the poll tax or any property disqualification. The Congregational Christian Churches and Evangelical and Reformed Church also urged the abolition of the poll tax.

Except for the resolutions supporting a permanent FEPC and the abolition of the poll tax, the pronouncements, by and large, appear to avoid the specific. Typically, the Methodists urge "equal opportunity in employment, up-grading in conditions of work; in exercise of the full rights of citizenship; in access to professional and business careers; in housing, in transportation, and in educational facilities"; and "equal protection through the agencies of law and order."[19] The Northern Baptists Convention delegates "dedicate ourselves and seek to commit our churches . . . that we actively work for equality in housing, education, economic opportunity in every field of honorable endeavor, and the unrestricted practice of the privileges and

---

[18] *Daily Christian Advocate* (Kansas City, Mo.: The Methodist Publishing House) , Vol. II, No. 7, p. 108 (May 3, 1944) .

[19] *Idem.*

responsibilities of free citizenship with full civil and religious liberty."[20]

These two quotations, general though they are, do make reference to a number of disabilities experienced by the Negro—housing, education, employment, transportation, citizenship—and to that extent they are a marked advance over the pronouncements of the previous decade.

The other statements on race relations in our national life dealt with a variety of topics. The Northern Baptists deplored the segregation of blood plasma; the Methodists and Northern Presbyterians called for a postwar settlement based on the principle of the equality of races; the Evangelical and Reformed and Presbyterians U.S.A. churches hammered away at lynching. The Presbyterian General Assembly was the only body to "oppose any discrimination against the Negro in the military services"[21] (1941), and in 1944 it commended "the War and Navy Departments upon the steps they have taken toward removing discrimination and segregation of Negroes in the armed forces, and affirm[ed] its continued hope that where practicable all such barriers will be removed."[22]

Segregation, practically unmentioned in the thirties, was touched on by two denominations in the early forties. We have already mentioned the Presbyterian U.S.A. deliverance on discrimination and segregation in the Armed Forces. In 1944 the General Assembly also ". . . declare[d] its conviction that discrimination and segregation on the basis of race, creed, or color in any form is undemocratic

---

[20] *Year Book of the Northern Baptist Convention, 1944* (Philadelphia: Judson Press), p. 275.

[21] *Minutes of the General Assembly of the Presbyterian Church in the United States of America, 1941* (Philadelphia: Office of the General Assembly) Part I, p. 164.

[22] *Minutes of the General Assembly of the Presbyterian Church in the United States of America, 1944* (Philadelphia: Office of the General Assembly) Part I, p. 233.

and unchristian. We recognize the great difficulty of overcoming all phases of this discrimination and segregation,
but we must not allow this difficulty to hinder progress
toward realizing this ideal."[23] The Evangelical and Reformed Church proclaimed in 1942: "We will seek to
eliminate from our own lives and through our influence
seek to free others from the embittering prejudices of
nationality, color, and creed. Remembering that in Christ
there are no such distinctions, we will lend our support to
efforts to eliminate from our institutions the evidences of
such prejudice—segregation, denial of civil rights, social
intolerance, and bestial lynching—so that brotherhood may
find a more perfect expression."[24]

The resolutions of the Southern Baptists during the
first five years of the forties, while still focusing on mob
violence, touched on such matters as more equitable economic and educational opportunities (1940 and 1941). In
1943 the report to the convention praised the "constructive Negro leadership" at the famous Conference of southern Negro leaders at Durham, North Carolina, October,
1942, and also the southern white leaders of the Atlanta
conference, April, 1943, who had admitted that the "Negro,
as an American citizen, is entitled to his civil rights and
economic opportunities."[25] The report frankly stated:
"What we seek is a *modus operandi* that will diminish
friction, eliminate injustices, and promote friendly co-
operation."[26]

The range of attitudes in this period on the place of the

---

[23] *Ibid.*, p. 232.

[24] *Acts and Proceedings of the Fifth Meeting of the General Synod of the
Evangelical and Reformed Church, 1942* (Cleveland: Central Publishing
House) , p. 264.

[25] *Annual of the Southern Baptist Convention, 1943,* printed and distributed by the Executive Committee of the Southern Baptist Convention, pp.
107-108. (Nashville, Tenn.)

[26] *Ibid.*, p. 107.

Negro in contemporary American society is completed with a pronouncement of the Southern Presbyterians:

> Still we need to acknowledge two obvious facts. The first is that decent, intelligent Negroes today are entitled to own or rent clean and comfortable homes, and to lead their lives in a pure, moral atmosphere. The second is that, even in the South, sentiment is changing as to the ethics or the wisdom of some of our present habits concerning racial separation. This shifting of sentiment is particularly noticeable among the youth of our churches. It behooves us as Christians to give patient study to our rules of conduct in order to make sure that we are justified in our actions as we sing:

> > "Join hands then, brothers of the faith,
> > Whate'er your race may be,
> > Who serves my Father as a son
> > Is surely kin to me."[27]

JIM CROW IN THE CHURCH

So much for the pronouncements dealing with conditions outside the churches. An outstanding recent characteristic is the growing trend toward self-examination. In fact more than one-third of the statements are focused on the church and its membership. They range from the Methodist recommendation that the Social Creed be read to congregations at least once a year or placed in their hands in printed form, to the Protestant Episcopal "Guiding Principles Designed to Govern the Church's Negro Work," calling for fellowship in worship and administration.

We cite here a part of the recommendations of the 1944 Methodist General Conference (See Appendix I C, page 130):

---

[27] *Minutes of the Eighty-Fourth General Assembly of the Presbyterian Church in the United States* (Richmond, Va.: Presbyterian Committee of Publication, 1944), p. 151.

Corporate Influence. Through the General Conferences, Annual Conferences, and similar church meetings, the Church should make its corporate influence felt against the collective evils of racism. It should seek to have interracial commissions appointed in nation, state, and every community where racial groups are to be found.

Education. Through conference, seminars, literature, church school and young people's classes, in laymen's groups, and in the Women's Society of Christian Service, the Church should seek to discover the mind of Christ in the field of race relations.

The Church in the Local Community. The minister and lay leader should seek to encourage within the official leadership of the local church a Christian attitude toward such community situations as involve the promotion of racial understanding and good will.[28]

Discrimination at national conventions (which some denominations had attempted to cope with in the thirties by adopting explicit policies) is another aspect of the churches' own affairs. The Protestant Episcopal Church in 1940 resolved that "the Committee on Arrangements for the next meeting of the General Convention strive to make arrangements that will allow the colored delegates and visitors to be accorded the same treatment as the white delegates."[29] In 1943 the Presbyterians U.S.A. stated that ". . . this General Assembly reiterates its testimony to the fundamental unity of humanity and its desire to practice Christian brotherhood in all matters relating to its meetings. . . ."[30] The Disciples of Christ in 1944 were so pleased by the way their no-discrimination policy of 1934 had worked that they adopted the following resolution on the treatment of Negro delegates:

---

[28] *Daily Christian Advocate*, p. 108.

[29] *Journal of the General Convention of the Protestant Episcopal Church in the United States of America, 1940*, p. 343.

[30] *Minutes of the General Assembly of the Presbyterian Church in the United States of America, 1943* (Philadelphia: Office of the General Assembly) Part I, pp. 201-202.

We commend the Committee on Arrangements of the 1944 International Convention at Columbus in securing the privileges of racial equality at the headquarters hotel. We believe that in the future, Committees on Arrangements for our International Convention should, insofar as possible, secure the privileges of social equality, and also seek to secure headquarters hotels where alcoholic beverages are not offered for sale.[31]

The Methodist Church on the other hand, at its 1944 General Conference, rejected this resolution of its Committee on State of the Church: "We recommend that committees arranging for general meeting of the Church seek to locate such meetings in places where entertainment can be provided without distinction on the basis of race."[32] (This action at the Methodist General Conference is considered in Chapter III.)

Another action of the same General Conference was the establishment of a Study Commission. After considerable debate, the following resolution was adopted:

Study Commission—We look to the ultimate elimination of racial discrimination within The Methodist Church. Accordingly, we ask the Council of Bishops to create forthwith a commission to consider afresh the relations of all races included in the membership of The Methodist Church and to report to the General Conference of 1948.[33]

The emphasis on self-examination as seen in these representative recommendations for study programs, interracial committees, observance of Race Relations Sunday and the like, reflected the practice of segregation by the

[31] *International Convention, Disciples of Christ,* 1944, (St. Louis, Mo.: Christian Board of Publication) , p. 339.

[32] *Daily Christian Advocate,* pp. 110-111.

[33] *Ibid.,* p. 108. The following amendment was also adopted: "We request the Council of Bishops to take into account the exceeding importance of providing in the nomination of the members of the commission . . . the most complete representation of all racial groups as possible." See *Proceedings,* p. 221. The Study Commission is discussed in Chapter III.

churches themselves. At least four communions, the Northern Baptist, Evangelical and Reformed, Presbyterian U.S.A., and Protestant Episcopal, in an action without precedent, issued statements that with varying emphases call for an end to Jim Crow in the church. And the Northern Presbyterians asked that their colleges admit Negroes and that their churches and colleges select teachers and leaders who are without prejudice.

Undoubtedly the most forthright and most advanced of all these denominational statements are the four principles adopted by the General Convention in 1943 of the Protestant Episcopal Church. In somewhat expanded form they have been adopted by the National Council of the same body as a set of "Guiding Principles Designed to Govern the Church's Negro Work":

WHEREAS, the following principles must be kept before us as the Christian goal, to-wit:
(1) Fellowship is essential to Christian worship;
(2) Fellowship is essential in Church administration;
(3) High standards must be maintained in every department of our work with the Negro; and
(4) It is both the function and the task of the Church to set the spiritual and moral goals for society, and to bear witness to their validity by achieving them in her own life;

... *Resolved* ... that this Convention commends the foregoing principles of Christian Social Relations to the clergy and laity of this Church as embodying a Christian approach to the New World Order.[34]

SINCE THE WAR

Race relations have maintained a central place in Protestant pronouncements. With the ending of the war new domestic issues arose at denominational conventions—in-

---

[34] *Journal of the General Convention of the Protestant Episcopal Church in the United States of America, 1943*, pp. 326-327.

dustrial relations, problems of church and state, amnesty for conscientious objectors, housing, compulsory military training. On the international scene there were resolutions on displaced persons, relief and reconstruction, UNESCO and other organizations of the United Nations. But inter-group relations continued to be a major concern.

In 1946 and 1947 resolutions were adopted which constitute a landmark in Protestant pronouncements on Negro-white relationships. The Federal Council of Churches at a special meeting in March of 1946 declared:

> The Federal Council of the Churches of Christ in America hereby renounces the pattern of segregation in race relations as unnecessary and undesirable and a violation of the Gospel of love and human brotherhood. Having taken this action, the Federal Council requests its constituent communions to do likewise. As proof of their sincerity in this renunciation they will work for a non-segregated Church and a non-segregated society.[35]

And the following denominations have adopted the statement as their own: Congregational Christian (1946), Disciples of Christ (1946 and 1947), Evangelical and Reformed (1947), and Presbyterian U.S.A. (1946 and 1947).

Three other denominations, the Brethren (1947), the United Presbyterians (1946 and 1947), and the Evangelical United Brethren (1946), without adopting the Federal Council statement, have recommended that their churches welcome Negroes. The Reformed Church in America (1946) raised the question of the compatibility of segregation and Christianity.

It is difficult to imagine anything more that many denominations can do in the way of *pronouncements* on the fundamental issue of segregation in the church.

To implement these resolutions several denominations

---

[35] *The Church and Race Relations, op. cit.,* p. 5.

are planning rather intensive programs. Most outstanding in this regard is the action of the Congregational Christian Churches to make race relations a major concern for the 1946-48 biennium:

A. The General Council of Congregational Christian Churches endorses the resolution of its Executive Committee taken in open meeting at Cleveland, Ohio, on January 31, 1946, calling for a major emphasis on race relations for the biennium of 1946-1948 and the co-ordination of the programs of the several Boards and agencies toward that end.

B. This biennial program of emphasis is to be concerned with relationships between *all* ethnic, religious, national, and cultural groups, combating not only the sins of racial and national pride but also of religious bigotry.

C. The Executive Committee of the General Council is authorized to establish a widely representative committee of lay people and ministers and to select its membership, which commitee shall forward this program of emphasis.

D. The Missions Boards and other national agencies of the denomination, the State Conferences, the Associations, and the local churches are urged to cooperate fully in this emphasis, using all the resources at our command to reach the conscience of each member of our Fellowship.[36]

The Evangelical and Reformed Church will make 1948-49 a period for special church-wide emphasis.

The Northern Presbyterians (1946) have authorized a study of how the denomination can achieve a non-segregated church. The Episcopalians (1946) requested the appointment of a

biracial committee . . . for the purpose of developing plans to stimulate increased participation of Negro laymen in the established program of the Church. This committee shall report its findings and recommendations to the Presiding Bishop and the National Council for appropriate action.[37]

---

[36] *Minutes, Eighth Regular Meeting, General Council of the Congregational Christian Churches of the United States* (New York: 1946) , p. 47.

[37] *Journal of the General Convention of the Protestant Episcopal Church in the United States of America, 1946,* p. 261.

The United Presbyterians (1947) have called for no discrimination in any meetings of the denomination and want the Synods to eliminate all vestiges of segregation in the Presbyteries.

The racial practices of denominational institutions have also been singled out. The Evangelical and Reformed Church (1947) is interested in its colleges and hospitals; the Congregationalists (1946), in their church-related colleges and schools; the Presbyterians U.S.A. (1946), in their seminaries and colleges; the Brethren (1947) and United Presbyterians (1947), in their colleges. The United Presbyterians have asked the church boards to establish scholarships in their colleges and youth conferences for minorities.

Fair employment practices legislation now has wide support in denominational pronouncement. The Northern Baptists (1946, 1947) endorse state legislation and want serious consideration given to federal legislation. The Presbyterians U.S.A. (1945) approve the New York State act and endorse a federal FEPC (1945, 1947). The Reformed Church in America (1945) commends the New York and New Jersey anti-discriminatory laws for fair employment. The Congregational (1946), Evangelical (1945), and Evangelical and Reformed (1947) conventions favored a federal FEPC.

Residential segregation, especially by means of restrictive covenants, has been denounced by the Northern Baptists (1946), Congregationalists (1946), Evangelical and Reformed (1947), and the United Presbyterians (1947).

In the denominations with a predominantly southern constituency there is a trend toward the specific in pronouncements. The Southern Presbyterians (1947) stress civil rights and condemn anti-minority groups. They also (1945) urge their churches to establish interracial committees in their communities and to promote opportunities for joint worship.

However, in 1946 the Southern Presbyterians adopted a resolution calling for a study to be made of the possibility of uniting all Negro Presbyterians in a Negro Presbyterian Church. At the 1947 General Assembly this proposal was not pressed.

The Southern Baptists in 1945, 1946, and 1947 adopted a series of resolutions favoring equal opportunity within the system of segregation. A committee appointed in 1946 reported to the 1947 convention:

The problem as we face it in our time is that of different races finding principles and methods of procedure that will insure justice to all and establish attitudes of mutual helpfulness and good-will.[38]

In a detailed report the committee reviewed the "work now being done by Southern Baptists among the Negroes of the South," described the "whole racial situation in its moral and religious aspects" with special reference to the responsibility of Baptists, and suggested a "charter of . . . Christian and Baptist principles and their necessary consequences in racial attitudes.[39]

SHORTCOMINGS

Has anything been overlooked in these pronouncements? They represent a great and gratifying advance in sensitivity and courage, and no reference to their shortcomings must obscure this fact of important gain.

The resolutions adopted by the annual conventions of the National Association for the Advancement of Colored People embody the principal demands of American Negroes. Using them as criteria one notes many things

---

[38] *Book of Reports, Southern Baptist Convention* (Nashville, Tenn.: Marshall & Bruce Company, 1947), p. 282.

[39] *Book of Reports, op. cit.*, pp. 280-284. Excerpts from this significant report are reproduced in the Appendix.

which Protestantism has either treated evasively or ignored entirely in its pronouncements. Take a few selected N.A.A.C.P. resolutions as illustrations:

1935: Discrimination in relief and work relief.
1936: Inclusion of agricultural and domestic workers under the Social Security Act. Discrimination in the Army and Navy. Discrimination and segregation in health and medical services.
1937: Segregation in low-cost housing. Stereotyping of Negroes by press, radio, and movies.
1938: Discrimination and segregation in parks, pools, educational centers, nursery schools.
1939: Discrimination and segregation by the Federal Housing Administration.[40]

One other problem has been on the "must" list of the N.A.A.C.P. since 1937—restrictive covenants. A restrictive covenant is ". . . an agreement by property owners in a neighborhood not to sell or rent their property to colored people for a definite period. . . ."[41] These agreements help to keep Negroes ". . . isolated from the main body of whites, and mutual ignorance helps reinforce segregative attitudes and other forms of race prejudice."[42] Myrdal believes, furthermore, that "the presence of a small scattering of upper and middle class Negroes in a white neighborhood . . . might serve to better race relations" and ". . . would contribute to property values in a neighborhood rather than cause them to deteriorate. The socially more serious effect of having segregation, however, is not to force this tiny group of middle and upper class Negroes to live among their own group, but to lay the Negro

---

[40] The complete texts of the resolutions adopted at the annual conventions are reported in *The Crisis*, Vol. 42, No. 8 (August, 1935), pp. 248-250; Vol. 43, No. 9 (September, 1936), pp. 277, 283; Vol. 44, No. 8 (August, 1937), pp. 246-248; Vol. 45, No. 9 (September, 1938), pp. 305-306; Vol. 46, No. 9 (September, 1939), pp. 280-282.

[41] Myrdal, Gunnar, *An American Dilemma*, I, p. 624.

[42] *Idem.*

masses open to exploitation and to drive down their housing standard even below what otherwise would be economically possible."[43]

Now it is significant that until 1946 not a single Protestant denomination had ever made a pronouncement on the subject of restrictive covenants. If the four denominations (Northern Baptist, Congregational Christian, Evangelical and Reformed, and United Presbyterian) cited on page 44 can really implement their denunciation of such practices, it will be a notable accomplishment since a great deal of the property where white Protestants live, especially in suburban areas, is so restricted. It is also believed that the denominations and especially their related institutions, such as colleges, own property or have endowments invested in property subject to covenants restricting the sale or lease to whites only.[44] More vital still is the relationship between restrictive covenants and the attendance and membership of Negroes in white congregations, which is so obvious that it hardly seems an exaggeration to say that until the churches are successful in abolishing restrictive covenants, their statements on fellowship in the church can hardly be realized.

The denominations have other blind spots. Only the Congregationalists have singled out the practice of their secondary schools. Only the Evangelical and Reformed Church has mentioned the policies and practices of its church-related hospitals. No denomination has ever mentioned such other church institutions as orphanages, homes for the aged, and settlement houses.

No denomination has called on those among its con-

---

[43] *Ibid.*, I, p. 625.

[44] See Alexander, Will W., "Our Conflicting Racial Policies," *Harper's Magazine*, Vol. 190, No. 1136 (January, 1945), p. 176. Some congregations have also been active in promoting restrictive covenants. See Long, Herman H., and Johnson, Charles S., *People vs. Property* (Nashville: Fisk University Press, 1947), pp. 82-83.

stituency who are in policy-making positions in business and industry to open to Negroes positions in occupations from which they usually are barred, such as clerks, salespersons, bookkeepers, stenographers, and other white-collar jobs.

How Effective Are Pronouncements?

Valuable as they are as standard-setters, pronouncements have the inherent limitation in that they are made, as a rule, not by the rank and file, but by a few persons whom special circumstances have subjected to liberalizing influences. The reader is warned, therefore, against concluding that the pronouncements mean more than they really do. The fact that in practically all cases they represent *minority* opinion, sometimes a very small minority, should be made clear. There is much variation, denomination by denomination, in this respect.

Dr. F. Ernest Johnson, writing in 1930 when the making of pronouncements had become the vogue "as codes of ethics (have been) among business and professional groups more recently" said:

. . . a set of pronouncements by denominational assemblies may be more or less remote from the thought of the rank and file of church members, not to mention their practice.

At the same time, some of the statements . . . represent much serious thought and careful consideration on the part of the bodies responsible for them. Others have less intrinsic authority or significance but are noteworthy because they have at least the weight of official declarations and may be used in educational work among the communions originating them.[45]

Dr. J. H. Oldham gives another use for pronouncements: "Authoritative statements of this kind may often be a strength and support to individual ministers in interpret-

---

[45] Johnson, F. Ernest, ed., *op. cit.*, p. 122.

ing the ethical implications of the gospel in face of criticism and opposition."[46]

Both Oldham and Johnson are critical of pronouncements "put over" by small minorities, with the result that it is not clear who are committed to them. Neither writer apparently believes that the statements have a very appreciable influence either on public opinion or even on the attitudes of the churches' members. As Johnson says: ". . . only when the church has given effect to its social convictions by incorporating them in its own discipline has its address to the community any social reality."[47]

Unless resolutions represent the honest convictions of the rank and file, "astute politicians . . . are quite capable of assessing the amount of real force which lies behind (them) and of attaching to them the weight that they deserve."[48] An illustration from a recent Georgia primary drives the point home. Roy Harris, campaign manager for Gene Talmadge, left the speech-making to Talmadge:

> Only once did he intervene in that department. That was when, for a brief moment, the Talmadge drive for race hatred threatened to backfire.
>
> Many clergymen and many church-going people in Georgia—too many for Harris' comfort—resented Talmadge's effort to set back the clock of racial tolerance. Many influential ministers preached that race hatred was un-Christian, and that hurt, for Georgians—particularly those in the Talmadge camp—are deeply religious. The drive began to take hold.
>
> But it stopped in its tracks when Harris went on the radio in a speech in which he branded the preachers of racial tolerance as hypocrites.
>
> "When those ministers are ready to open their churches to

---

[46] Oldham, J. H., in Visser 't Hooft, W. A., and Oldham, J. H., *The Church and its Functions in Society* (Chicago: Willet, Clark & Company, 1937) , p. 207.

[47] Johnson, F. Ernest, *The Church and Society* (New York: Abingdon Press, 1935) , p. 94.

[48] Oldham, J. H., *op. cit.*, p. 208.

Negroes and seat them beside whites," he said, "I will listen to them. Until then, they are not worth listening to."

It was a challenge the ministers could not meet. Their congregations were willing to listen to and endorse arguments for Negro rights, as long as they didn't come too close. Harris knew what he was doing. The "Christian" angle all but disappeared from the anti-Talmadge campaign.[49]

SUMMARY

Gradually over the past forty years Protestantism has become sensitive to America's race problem. After the first World War it condemned lynchings and brutality; during the depression it called for equal opportunity; with World War II came the recognition of racial discrimination in economic, political, and civic affairs. Since World War II, Protestant pronouncements have spoken for the growing ranks of those who believe that the heart of the problem of Negro-white relations is segregation—in employment, in education, in housing—and in the church. There is little evidence yet that the convictions of the rank-and-file membership of Protestant denominations are greatly influenced by these official actions.

Although a number of important interracial issues remain on which the churches have not yet chosen to speak, the unbiased observer cannot fail to be impressed by the revolutionary progress made by liberal leaders in Protestantism during and since World War II in getting a prophetic note into the record.

---

[49] Roth, Robert, "Georgia Liberals Botched Their Campaign to Beat Talmadge for Governor," *Philadelphia Record*, September 11, 1946, p. 12.

CHAPTER 3

What the Churches Do:
Nationally and Regionally

THE CRUCIAL test of the churches' attitudes toward the
Negro is to be found in the actual practices of local congregations. Most church bodies have always recognized this
fact as a matter of course. It is not so clear, however, that
they have always been aware that inconsistencies between
precept and practice continue to extend right up from the
local to the regional and national levels. To obtain a picture of the larger pattern of Negro-white relationships it
is important to examine the churches' racial policies and
practices with respect to ecclesiastical structure and denominational conventions. At the national and regional
level the denominations are presumably less bound by
local custom and are, therefore, in a better position to put
into practice the convictions voiced by the pronouncements at national conventions.

Probably 8,300,000 of the 14,000,000 Negroes in the
United States belong to some Christian church. Approximately 8,000,000 are Protestants and 300,000 are Roman
Catholics. Of this 8,000,000, approximately 7,500,000 are
in separate Negro denominations.[1] The remaining 500,000
are members of Negro churches in predominantly white
denominations.

---

1 Statistics of religious bodies are notoriously unreliable. See the discussion of this point in Benson Y. Landis, ed., *Yearbook of American Churches,*
1945, p. 143. Our figure of 8,000,000 Negro Protestants expresses in round
numbers the total inclusive church memberships of the National Baptist

DENOMINATIONS WITH NEGRO CHURCHES

At the national level, with the exception of The Methodist Church and the Disciples of Christ, Negro churches in predominantly white denominations experience no segregation. In the regional and local bodies, such as Synods and Presbyteries, Negro churches (with certain exceptions) are also included and have representation—outside of the South.

TABLE I

MEMBERSHIP IN NEGRO CHURCHES IN PREDOMINANTLY WHITE DENOMINATIONS AFFILIATED WITH THE FEDERAL COUNCIL OF CHURCHES[2]

DENOMINATION	TOTAL U.S.A. MEMBERSHIP	NEGRO Churches	NEGRO Members
Northern Baptist	1,555,914	232	45,000
Congregational Christian	1,075,401	230	19,374
Disciples of Christ	1,672,354	500	60,000
Methodist	8,046,129	3,115	330,600
Presbyterian U. S.	565,853	54	3,132
Presbyterian U. S. A.	2,040,399	410	40,581
Protestant Episcopal	2,227,524	347	60,326
United Lutheran	1,690,204	5	1,774
United Presbyterian	193,637	13	1,166

Formal structure can be very deceptive. The types of relationships between Negro and white denominational brothers in the local, regional, and national bodies are an area in need of investigation. In our broad over-all introductory survey we are forced to speak tentatively as to the degree of integration or segregation in the various denominational organizations.[3]

Convention, U.S.A., Inc., National Baptist Convention of America, African Methodist Episcopal Church, African Methodist Episcopal Zion Church, and Colored Methodist Episcopal Church as given in Landis, *op. cit.,* pp. 144, 147. (Thus we have not included the smaller sects.)

[2] The number of Negro churches and Negro members has been secured from denominational headquarters. Total U.S.A. membership figures are from Landis, *op. cit.,* p. 89. No Negro churches are affiliated with the Southern Baptist Convention, the Friends General Conference or the six other members of the Federal Council of Churches which we investigated.

[3] The analysis of ecclesiastical structure is based on information secured

DENOMINATIONS WHICH SEGREGATE

The Disciples of Christ illustrates what we have in mind by the deceptiveness of formal structure. Negro Disciples churches are organized in a National Christian Missionary Convention which, in theory, is not racial but in practice is so. In 1945, the Negro work was organized on a new basis with an executive committee made up of twelve Negroes representing their convention and nine representatives of the United Christian Missionary Society (white) and other agencies and boards of the Disciples. Practically, all activities are carried on on a separate basis. Few Negroes are on the national boards although in recent years there has been a movement toward more equitable representation.

On the regional level almost all Negro congregations in The Methodist Church in the United States, regardless of location, are in the Central Jurisdiction.[4] Though separate, these Negro Methodist churches, through the Central Jurisdiction, are said to have full representation on the same basis as other jurisdictions in the General Conference and all of its Boards, Committees, and secretarial staffs.

Presbyterian U.S.A. Negro churches in the South, outside of the State of Kentucky, are in separate Synods and Presbyteries. In other parts of the country they are in the general Synods and Presbyteries. For the Southern Presbyterians (U.S.) we find forty-eight Negro churches in separate

---

through the original questionnaire addressed to denominational executives, and correspondence and interviews with persons intimately acquainted with church organization.

[4] White Methodist churches are organized according to their geographical location into five jurisdictions. At least one white organization in recent years has challenged the Jim-crow arrangements in the Methodist Church. "The Detroit Methodist Conference, in the first action of its kind in the history of this denomination, invited Negro ministers and their congregations into full membership and fellowship." Embree, Edwin R., in Sperry, Willard L., ed. *Religion and Our Racial Tensions* (Cambridge: Harvard University Press, 1945) , p. 56.

Synods and six churches not in separate Synods. The United Presbyterians have one Presbytery in Tennessee which is composed entirely of colored congregations. Their only other colored congregation, Witherspoon, is in Indiana Presbytery. Both of these Presbyteries, however, are in the Second Synod, where representatives of the colored congregations are reported to be treated on an equal basis with the white representatives of other congregations.[5]

The Congregational Christian Negro Churches are also in separate bodies in the South. Outside of the South there is no separation.

Denominations Which Integrate

Negro churches which are members of the Northern Baptist Convention are included in the Baptist associations at all levels—national, state, and local.

The five Negro congregations in the United Lutheran Church in America, all located in the North, are also included in all Lutheran associations.

In the Protestant Episcopal Church all Negro churches are integrated in all the regional organizations, including the South. Proposals have been made by Southerners to establish a separate organization of Negro churches in the South, but these have been rejected by the General Convention. Some of the southern Negro churches, however, have felt that they do not have equitable representation in diocesan conventions.[6]

---

[5] In 1947 the United Presbyterian General Assembly adopted a resolution urging the Synods to redefine the boundaries of their Presbyteries to avoid segregation. The Northern Presbyterians (1946, 1947) made a similar request.

[6] According to *Events and Trends in Race Relations, a Monthly Summary* . . . "white Episcopalians of Georgia have voted to seat Negro Episcopal clergymen and lay delegates with full rights in future diocesan conventions. The Georgia Episcopalians are the next to the last state group to approve the anti-discrimination amendment to the diocesan constitution. South Carolina is the only state which has failed to adopt the amendment."

THE METHODIST ARRANGEMENT

The Methodist Church, with a total inclusive membership of 8,046,129 and a membership in Negro churches of 330,600, is the largest Protestant denomination in the United States. The Methodist Church has more Negro churches and more Negro members than all of the other "white" Protestant denominations combined.

The Methodist Church's "Plan of Union" had little effect on the existing racial relationships on the regional or local level. The Northern branch of Methodism included Negro churches in a few of its conferences, for example, New York and New England. Most Negro Methodist Episcopal churches, including those in the Southern branch, were in separate conferences. Today the pattern at the conference level throughout the whole country remains as it was before union. Union, in the opinion of some observers, brought some retrogression. Formerly, all Negro churches did belong to the General Conference of the northern church. Today, even northern Negro churches are segregated along with all other Negro churches in the Central Jurisdiction. On the other hand, there are Methodist "liberals" who say that union was not a backward step racially since all jurisdictions, including the Negro Central Jurisdiction, are included and represented proportionately in the General Conference—the national convention of The Methodist Church which meets every four years.

At the 1944 General Conference the Committee on State of the Church brought to the conference a report on "Conditions of Peace." One section, proposing a study com-

---

Vol. IV, Number 11 (June, 1947) p. 345. Actually there are two dioceses in South Carolina. The Diocese of Upper South Carolina voted in 1945 to give full representation to Negroes of the diocese. The Diocese of South Carolina (Charleston Convocation) in April, 1947 endorsed this policy but this has not as yet been voted upon and approved.

mission, touched a sore spot in the Methodist organism. The committee had said:

> We look to the ultimate elimination of racial discrimination within The Methodist Church. Accordingly, we ask the Council of Bishops to create forthwith a commission to consider afresh the relations of all races included in the membership of The Methodist Church and to report to the General Conference of 1948.[7]

The stenographic report of the ensuing debate, too lengthy for inclusion here, provides an enlightening cross-section of contemporary Methodist sentiment.[8] The resolution was finally adopted, but the commission was not appointed until more than a year elapsed. As far as can be determined, furthermore, the commission has yet to appoint an executive secretary.

WHAT HAPPENS AT CONVENTIONS

Though Negro churchmen have little association with white churchmen, as is evident from the structure of American society and the structure of the Protestant Church, there is one occasion, at least, when Negro leadership in the "white" denominations—clergymen and laymen—have the opportunity and privilege of meeting with their white denominational brothers. The denominational conventions and assemblies provide this common ground. Some denominations have national meetings every year, for example, the Presbyterian bodies, the Baptist, and Disciples; the Congregationalists and Lutherans meet every two years; the Episcopalians every three years; and the Methodists, every four years.[9]

---

[7] *Proceedings, Forty-first General Conference of The Methodist Church, 1944,* p. 170.

[8] *Ibid.,* pp. 170-173, 219-221.

[9] Different Boards and Commissions, having Negro representation, meet in the interim between general meetings.

In the 1920's, spurred on by the Y.M.C.A., the Y.W.C.A., the Federal Council of Churches, and other national bi-racial and interracial organizations, efforts were made to have denominational national conventions and assemblies conducted in such a way that Negroes would not experience humiliation.

In 1931 the Federal Council of Churches adopted the following set of principles with respect to the provision of accommodations for Negro delegates and visitors by the convention hotel:

In making arrangements for hospitality for an interracial conference through either a national or a local committee with the hotels, it should be borne in mind that the entertainment is for all delegates without discrimination. Agreement should be sought covering the following:

(a) No segregation of specific groups in room assignments.
(b) No discrimination against any delegates in the use of hotel entrances, lobbies, elevators, dining rooms and other hotel service or facilities.
(c) Specific instruction of hotel employees by the hotel authorities regarding the interracial character of the conference and the treatment of all delegates with equal courtesy.[10]

Not all of the denominations in the Federal Council (nor the Southern Baptists and the Friends General Conference) have Negro churches or Negro members in "white" churches. Thus one could not expect to find that every denomination has adopted a policy of no discrimination at the national meetings. And such is the case. The Church of the Brethren, the Evangelical Church, the Evangelical and Reformed Church, Five Years Meeting of Friends, Reformed Church in America, United Brethren in Christ, Southern Baptist Convention, and Friends General Conference have no Negro churches, extremely few Negro

---

[10] The Federal Council of Churches of Christ in America, *Annual Report* (New York, 1931), pp. 112-113.

members, and no official convention policy. The Five Years Meeting of Friends and the Reformed Church in America report that they have an administrative policy of no discrimination. This is not to imply that all the other denominations mentioned above do not provide entertainment without discrimination for an occasional colored guest. Probably most of them do treat Negro visitors without discrimination.

The Southern Baptist Convention "*per se* does not consider the Negro Baptists who live in the same territory as in any way part and parcel of their denominational life . . . it does not recognize the existence of 'sins of caste,' as they have been called, that exist within the framework of segregation. Nevertheless, the 'Negro Brethren' are recognized as living within the same area and as having a common tradition."[11] The Southern Baptist Convention provides a segregated section for Negro Baptists who bring fraternal messages to the convention.

Of those denominations with Negro churches, the Congregational Christian, Disciples of Christ, Northern Baptist, and Protestant Episcopal have stated that when making arrangements for conferences involving racial groups care should be taken that there be no discrimination. The United Presbyterians and the United Lutherans state that they administratively carry out an inclusive policy.

The Northern Presbyterians have no stated policy. They apparently have had difficulties—as at the General Assembly in Detroit, 1943—in carrying out their administrative policy of no discrimination.[12]

The Presbyterian Church in the United States, having a constituency entirely made up of Southerners, shows the

---

[11] McClain, Howard, "Program of the Southern Baptist Convention in Race Relations from 1939-1944" (Unpublished MSS), p. 2.

[12] Fey, Harold E., in "News of the Christian World," *Christian Century*, Vol. LX, No. 23 (June 9, 1943), pp. 697, 702.

influence of regional custom in bold relief. At the 1944 General Assembly on its own conference grounds at Montreat, North Carolina, Negro commissioners sat by themselves at a separate table in the hotel dining room—and slept in a separate building.

THE METHODIST COMPROMISE

The Methodists adopted at their 1944 General Conference a policy of "adequate and suitable" entertainment for all delegates. At this meeting in Kansas City, the second general conference of the united Methodist Church, "Negro delegates were subjected to shabby treatment. . . . They had great difficulty in securing food since the color line was drawn sharply by hotels and restaurants. The local committee struggled with the problem, but with indifferent success."[13]

The situation was so bad that the bishops held a conference and Bishop G. Bromley Oxnam apologized for the treatment of Negro delegates. He said a committee was working on it and that for the entire Council of Bishops ". . . it is our firm resolve to do all in our power to see that such provision shall be made in the future that this situation shall never happen again."[14]

In an attempt to make certain that such a situation would never happen again, the Committee on State of the Church, Ernest Fremont Tittle, Chairman, brought to the convention the following resolution: "We recommend that committees arranging for general meetings of the Church seek to locate such meetings in places where entertainment can be provided without distinction on the basis of race."[15] The chairman said that this ". . . is a resolution that is

---

[13] *Zion's Herald*, Vol. CXXII, No. 20 (May 17, 1944), p. 311.

[14] *Proceedings, Forty-first General Conference of the Methodist Church, 1944*, p. 64.

[15] *Ibid.*, p. 168.

covered not as a mandate, but as a moral and religious directive."[16]

To Tittle's recommendation calling for no discrimination, John E. Stevens of the North Mississippi Conference moved the following substitute amendment: "We recommend that the Committees arranging for general meetings of the Church locate such meetings only in places where adequate and suitable entertainment can be provided for all delegates and representatives of the Church."[17]

Two excerpts from the debate show something of the range in attitudes in The Methodist Church. Thelma Stevens, Executive Secretary of Christian Social Relations and Local Church Action of the Women's Division of Christian Service of the Board of Missions and Church Extension, speaking for the original motion, said:

. . . The Christian Church has lagged far behind in its social thinking and in its social courage and planning and I would wish for this great Methodist Church of ours that we might step out on this issue and step out with so much conviction that we would be able to do the thing that we know is right to do. We keep talking about this thing, we keep trying to do something about it, but every time something is suggested that we do it we lose our courage. . . .

I take it for granted that those of you who are in this body have been elected by your Conferences to represent that group and to report that group effectively and I am sure that this great Methodist membership of ours would want us to take the stand that is right on this issue that is very important now as we are looking toward a new world. We thought today and yesterday in terms of great plans for building a better world and one of the best places to start to build a world of fellowship and good will is within our own body, within our own group, and this would simply be one small gesture in that direction.

Replied W. Marvette Curtis (Alabama):

---

16 *Ibid.,* p. 167.
17 *Ibid.,* p. 168.

. . . Don't move us so fast! . . . We would maybe in the next thirty or forty years move a little faster.

. . . but I was born where they had fifteen colored people to every white man, and I am not going to talk about that. I helped and stood back of the Constitutional Amendment in Alabama that we might have a fair electorate in 1901 and the race issue was in many things down there! I love the race of coal-black color. My old black mammy nursed me.[18]

The original resolution was defeated and the amendment adopted.

WANTED: MORE KNOWLEDGE

Even when denominations have policies (explicit or implicit) of equal treatment for all delegates, it is no simple matter to put these intentions into practice. Thus the Disciples of Christ have a stated policy of no segregation, but they were frank to admit that Negro delegates experienced discrimination at the convention hotel and dining room, as well as at other hotels in Columbus, Ohio, January 22 to 29, 1944.[19]

The policies and practices of regional and local associations are not known by denominational headquarters. One can safely assume that in the South the practice is not likely to be one of integration, but in other sections of the country also Negro delegates experience discrimination and segregation. As the reporter for the Disciples wrote: "State conventions lag far behind the International Convention." How far, nobody knows. There are literally hundreds of regional and local meetings whose policies and practices in even a single denomination no one yet has investigated. It is not our intention to over-simplify this problem. A reply to our questionnaire from the Congregationalists shows some of the difficulties:

---

18 *Ibid.*, pp. 168-169.
19 Reply to questionnaire. But remember their pronouncement at the same conference. (See p. 40.)

However, state or regional conference meetings are not subject to national agency policies, and vary according to conference. We do not have the data to enable us to report for the 35 conferences. We presume the patterns vary. New York State Conference, e.g., always clears with the hotel about non-discrimination; but at the 1944 meeting in Syracuse, when an overflow of delegates led to use of an additional hotel, one of our Negro pastors was refused a room. Conference officials expressed their concern but had not made arrangements in advance at the second hotel, and could do nothing but find private lodging for the pastor concerned.[20]

In spite of these evidences of discrimination in northern states, no denomination, as far as I know, has ever taken a case of racial discrimination to court under a state civil rights law.[21]

As an indication of some of the more advanced thought with regard to interracial meetings, there is the report of the Friends General Conference, composed of six Yearly Meetings.

No discrimination whatever in any arrangements of the conference itself; Friends General Conference 1944 and earlier (Cape May, N. J.) secured community's special permission for colored minority attenders to come to Young People's dances on pier, and to use one beach ordinarily reserved for white people.

Arrangements committee for Friends General Conference 1946 has not yet met. Question may be brought up, we think, as to whether Friends should be content to have only fraction of beach open, or to use hotels that might (if we asked the question) refuse to accommodate some of our guests.

The occasional minority member, and the much larger number of guest speakers, discussion leaders, etc. have been entertained at certain hotels where many of our white attenders also stay. The issue has not been tried at certain other hotels used by white attenders. Possibly discrimination has been avoided.[22]

---

[20] Reply to questionnaire.

[21] For an account of a CIO test case of discrimination by a Columbus,

This view does not prevail among all Friends. At a meeting of the American Friends Fellowship Council in 1945 in Indianapolis, Indiana, Negroes were not invited to a dinner served at the First Friends Church. A few delegates expressed their concern over the incident by refusing to attend the dinner meeting.

Summary

To the best of my knowledge, the facts presented on ecclesiastical structure and denominational conventions are accurate, but at the present time, even at the national level, the details of the patterns of Negro-white relationships are somewhat blurred. Of the regional and local patterns less is known. What is needed is a series of intensive studies of denominational practices, nationally and regionally.

This we do know. Segregation is a characteristic of the Protestant Church. Most Negro Protestants are in separate denominations. Methodist and Disciples Negro churches are in separate organizations. Presbyterian and Congregational Negro churches are in separate organizations in the South. Baptist, Lutheran, and Episcopal Negro churches experience no organizational segregation.

The ground for hope lies in the announced policies of nearly all denominations to eliminate discrimination at denominational conventions, and in the pronouncements calling for the elimination of segregation in church organization and administration.

Ohio, hotel, see *Events and Trends in Race Relations, a Monthly Summary,* Vol. IV, No. 9 (April, 1947), p. 271.

[22] Reply to questionnaire.

CHAPTER 4

What the Churches Do: Locally

APPROXIMATELY seven and a half million Protestant Negroes are in "Negro" denominations and a half million Negroes are in separate Negro churches in the "white" denominations. How many Negroes are in predominantly white local churches? Does Protestantism have any policy with respect to "open" membership in local churches? These questions we shall hope to answer in this chapter.

EACH LOCAL CHURCH A LAW TO ITSELF

Protestantism in general has no *stated* policy with respect to mixed membership. Statements like the following can be taken as fairly expressing the policy, such as it is, of all seventeen of the bodies on which we are reporting: "The denomination has no formulated policy in this matter, but allows each congregation to set its own policy," or, "Policy is made by the local congregation. In general Negroes are not received. No law against it. But social custom is the strongest law."

The actual policy of Protestantism, then, seems to be to leave the question of Negro membership to the local congregation. However, during the past few years many denominations have touched on this ticklish question. Recognizing that most church members are unaware that segregation is unchristian, the denominations have attempted to raise the question of the compatibility of Christianity and segregation.

That this interest is both recent and probably confined to a small group within Protestantism would seem to be borne out by the fact that the denominational headquarters can furnish the names of only a handful of churches known to have Negro or other colored American members (Japanese-Americans, Chinese-Americans, American Indians, Mexicans, Koreans, Filipinos, Puerto Ricans). Some officers at denominational headquarters do not know of a single instance of a mixed congregation. Others name three or four "downtown" churches in large metropolitan areas attended by a few Negroes or other colored Americans. The paucity of data on congregational membership at headquarters illustrates the inadequacy of the denominations' present policies toward the integration of the Negro.

WHAT THE LOCAL CHURCHES DO

This lack of information is all the more significant because surveys of six denominations made in connection with this study brought to light scores of Protestant churches with some Negro members.[1]

---

[1] I am trying to evaluate the church as a whole, not the work of the exceptional individual on a denominational board or in a local church. I personally share the values for which many of these individuals are working; in fact, I am now engaged in a denominational social action project in race-relations. Such "extracurricular activities" of some denominations, however, can easily be overemphasized.

I am deeply indebted to officers of the Congregational Christian Churches, the Northern Baptist Convention, the United Presbyterian Church, the Evangelical and Reformed Church, the Church of the Brethren, and the Protestant Episcopal Church, and to the Race Relations Division of the American Missionary Association for assistance in collecting data regarding local churches in those denominations with more than one racial group in attendance or membership. The method was as follows:

Postcards worded as follows were mailed to nearly eighteen thousand ministers in six denominations: "From many sources we are having inquiries as to the practices of the local churches with respect to race relations. We have no way of knowing how many of our churches have members of more than one nationality or racial group. Will you please help us secure this information by *underscoring* which of the groups listed below are represented in your church membership, attendance, Sunday School, young people's society, or other organizations: Caucasian, Negro, American Indian, Japanese-American, Chinese-American, Korean, Mexican, Puerto Rican. Minister .... Address ...."

Among the 6,356 ministers who replied were 860 who said that Negroes

To quote Charles S. Johnson, this information was an "extraordinary revelation."[2]

Congregational Christian Churches

Consider first the Congregational Christian churches. Nearly four hundred reported one or more persons of color in the attendance or membership of white congregations. Half of these churches had Negroes in membership or attendance, the remainder having Japanese-Americans, Chinese-Americans, Mexicans, and so on. Fuller information from eighty-one of the "white" churches with Negro members showed 337 Negro members and 399 attendants. Just two churches, however, one in Lawrence, Massachusetts, and one in South Berkeley, California, accounted for over half of these colored participants. Only these two by any stretch of the imagination can be called interracial. In the remaining seventy-nine churches there were but 208 attendants and 115 members. Ten of these are "inclusive" only in their Sunday Schools or Daily Vacation Bible Schools.

---

took part in some way in the life of their churches. To them was sent a questionnaire that dealt primarily with the degree of minority group integration and the characteristics of the church membership and neighborhood. The minister was asked to state the number of Negro members who attend or are members of the congregation, their participation in church organizations such as Sunday School, women's organizations, young people's society, board of control, and so on. Other questions asked about the occupations of the membership, the racial composition of the neighborhood, and the attitudes of church members and the board of control toward minority group people. The minister was asked to tell the story of how the church came to be inclusive. Table II shows the extent of this inquiry and the facts it turned up about Negro participation in predominantly white churches. The data are summarized by States in Appendix II A. The reader is cautioned against thinking of these as "complete" figures or as "representative" figures. What they really show is that Negroes, in small numbers, take part in the life of churches in many parts of the country.

[2] "The most notable item of the month which concerns the Church is the extraordinary revelation, from a survey of two major denominations, that a larger percentage of the churches than was expected, or suspected, had opened the doors of membership to one or more persons of other than the white race." Johnson, Charles S., *Events and Trends in Race Relations, A Monthly Summary*, Vol. II, No. 7 (February, 1945), p. 184.

TABLE II

NEGRO PARTICIPATION IN PREDOMINANTLY WHITE CHURCHES OF SIX DENOMINATIONS

DENOMINATION	CARDS TO MINISTERS			QUESTIONNAIRES TO INCLUSIVE CHURCHES			NUMBER OF NEGROES IN WHITE CHURCHES	
						White Churches with Negro Partici-		
	Sent	Returned	Negro Underlined	Sent	Returned	pation	Attenders	Members
Congregational Christian ..	3,800	1,504	197	197	109	81	399	337
Northern Baptist	5,300	1,050	166	166	99	80	236	149
United Presbyterian	850	544	20	20	14	10	19	15
Evangelical and Reformed .	2,850	743	6	6	3	1	1	0
Church of the Brethren ...	1,100	561	6	6	4	2	7	3
Protestant Episcopal	4,000	1,954	465	465	160	116	470	816
Total	17,900	6,356	860	860	389	290	1,132	1,320

See Appendix II for additional details.

This, then, is the general pattern: If there are Negroes
in the local churches at all, they are in very small and in-
conspicuous numbers. And as we shall presently see, if there
are *many* Negroes in the neighborhood, there are probably *none* in the "white" church. The Negro-white pattern
of church membership and participation is essentially like
the larger community pattern. If there are a very few
Negroes in the neighborhood, integration may occur. If
there are many, segregation usually occurs, both in the
neighborhood and in the church.

Analysis of information from all of the 386 Congregational Christian Churches reporting non-white minority
persons in their congregations showed a majority of them
to be in small towns or "socially close-knit city neighborhoods" with one to three non-white families. Several are
in areas where non-white participation is usually "inter-
mittent and temporary."[3]

In churches with a few Negro members the relationships
tend to be friendly. Wrote a Connecticut minister:

> Our "problem" is not acute. We have a few Negroes in our
> town, and all the churches are open to them. We have only
> two families in our church. The real division in our community
> is between Protestant English and French Catholics—both
> white.

And a Massachusetts minister:

> The Negro family came into our fellowship because many
> years ago the Negro grandmother worked for a fine old New
> England family here in the city. When she married, the family
> came to the Church School and now the grandchildren are in
> the school. The congregation accepts them, treats them cour-
> teously and in a friendly manner.

---

[3] L. Maynard Catchings, *The Participation of Racial and Nationality
Minority Peoples in Congregational-Christian Churches* (Mimeographed:
Department of Race Relations, American Missionary Association Division,
The Board of Home Missions, Congregational-Christian Churches, 1946),
p. 9.

In five churches, four in Massachusetts and one in Connecticut, the ministers' replies indicated that the Negro members are well integrated: In Charlestown, Massachusetts, one of the two Negro attenders and members is Sunday School superintendent and the other is president of the women's society. There are two Negro attenders and four Negro members in a Cohasset, Massachusetts, church. One is president of the women's society and another is an officer in the young people's society. A Negro is superintendent of the Sunday School of a Boston, Massachusetts, church which has 15 Negro attenders and 11 Negro members. Three Negro families attend the church in Harvard, Massachusetts. A Negro is superintendent of the Sunday School, and the women's society has a Negro member. In Madison, Connecticut, six Negroes attend and ten are members. A Negro is president of the young people's society.[4]

Northern Baptist Convention

Three hundred and sixty-seven churches in the Northern Baptist Convention reported one or more persons of color in attendance or membership, 166 with Negroes and 201 without Negroes (Japanese, Indians, etc.). Fuller information from eighty of these Baptist churches showed that there were about 236 Negroes in attendance and 149 Negro members.

One hundred forty-nine Negro members divided among eighty churches is less than two per church.

Eight of the churches reported a few Negro children in Sunday School but no members. Two others had Negro children in Daily Vacation Bible Schools but no members. One had a Negro in the Boy Scouts, but no members. In one church the Negro caretaker attended but was not a

---

[4] Negroes form 1.7%, 1.1%, 1.7%, .7%, and .3% respectively of the population of these communities.

member, and in another church there were Negro attenders in the summer only, but no members.

In five churches the data supplied by the minister indicated that the Negro members are well integrated. Thus, in a rural church in upstate New York (Cuba) that has three Negro attenders and four members there are two Negroes in the women's organization. Another New York church in a small city of 10,000 people (Oneida), of whom twenty-six are Negroes, has three attenders and seven members: two are in the women's society and one is a teacher. In a small town in Michigan (Howell) the two Negro attenders and members attend the church dinners. In a Massachusetts city of 50,000 (Leominster), with a Negro population of fifty, there are two Negroes in the women's society and the congregation is reported to be seeking more Negro members. A "white" Baptist church also in Massachusetts (Lowell), has two Negroes on its board of control. This church of 1,000 members has thirty Negro attenders and forty Negro members, ten of whom are in the women's society, twelve in the men's society, five in the choir, and four in the young people's society.

Most of the communities in which these eighty churches are located are rural places in which only a few Negroes live. The following proportions of Negroes to the total population are typical: in Eldon, Iowa, 1 to 1,676; Cuba, New York, 4 to 1,699; North Wales, Pa., 45 to 2,450; Woodstock, Vt., 15 to 2,512. Approximately five-sixths of the eighty churches are located in communities under 100,000 population. In large cities (100,000 or more people) only sixty Negroes were reported in "white" church activities, and thirty of these are in the Lowell church. This city has a population of 101,000.

United Presbyterian Church

Seventy-three United Presbyterian churches reported

"inclusive" congregations, twenty of which had one or more Negroes.

In the ten churches from which fuller information was obtained were nineteen attenders and fifteen members, an average of about two Negro attenders and one member per church. The pattern of location of these ten United Presbyterian churches follows very closely the distribution characteristic of the Congregational Christian and Northern Baptist churches. The majority are in small communities where extremely few Negroes live.

Comments made by ministers supplying the information are particularly illuminating:

Turtle Creek, Penna. (no attendants, 2 members):
  Members' children dropped out at high school age.
Harrisville, Ohio (1 attendant, 1 member):
  Two are in the Sunday School, 1 in the Young People's Society. Congregation is cool toward church membership and membership in the women's society.
Americus, Kansas (2 attendants, no members):
  Negro janitor.
Darlington, Penna. (1 attendant, 3 families are members):
  No Negro church.
Latrobe, Penna. (2 attendants, 2 members):
  Wife is second generation of family in church.
  Two Negro churches in the town.
Monmouth, Illinois:
  Children attend Daily Vacation Bible School.
Pittsburgh, Penna.:
  Children (number not given) attending services are from a correctional school.
Ottawa, Kansas (3 attendants, no members):
  Welcomed in worship service, but encouraged to attend own church six blocks away.
San Diego, Cal. (10 attendants, number of members not given):
  War Housing Project. Many Negroes attend Bible classes. Average worship attendance of all people—100.
Brooklyn, N. Y. (number of attendants not given, 4 members):
  Two Negroes in Young People's Society, 1 Negro holds office. People would resent more Negroes in membership.

Evangelical and Reformed Church

Nearly 3,000 inquiries directed to local churches in the Evangelical and Reformed Church brought information about *only six churches* attended by one or more Negroes.

Apparently there were no Negro members. Again the comments were instructive: Negro children in Daily Vacation Bible School and Scouts; mother and two children attend rarely; one Negro formerly attended Young People's Society, but discontinued when she grew up and became self-conscious.

Church of the Brethren

Among 1,100 local churches in the Church of the Brethren only two could be found with Negro participants.

These two reported a total of seven Negro attenders and three Negro members. In one of the churches, located near a seminary, a Negro is in the men's organization and a Negro is in the Young People's Society.

Protestant Episcopal Church

The rectors of 465 out of 4,000 Protestant Episcopal Churches reported some Negro participation. Fuller information from 116 of these showed them to have approximately 470 Negro attenders and 816 Negro members.

The vast majority of the 116 churches are in the North; for example, twenty-seven are in New York, twenty-five in Massachusetts, eight each in California, Connecticut, New Jersey, and Pennsylvania, six in Ohio, and so on. Only five white churches with Negro participants are in southern and border states (Delaware, Kentucky, Louisiana, Oklahoma, and Virginia), each with one Negro attender and one Negro member. None of these southern churches reported Negroes participating in social organizations.

In most of the 116 churches the number of Negroes attending the worship service or Sunday School was very small. One church in Worcester, Massachusetts, however, had a membership of 100 Negroes, and an attendance of 145; and a "downtown" Brooklyn church had thirty-five Negro attenders and ninety members. These two are obviously exceptions.

In comparison with other denominations, however, there is a sizeable number of "white" churches in which Negroes participate in social organizations. In at least forty-three churches one or more Negroes are members of some social organization, and in approximately twenty-five churches they seem to be unusually well integrated.

The women's societies of twenty-six churches report Negro members. Ten have Negroes in the men's organizations. Nineteen have Negro choir members. The young people's societies of eleven churches have Negro members. In three churches Negroes are on the boards of control or vestry. One church accepted the services of a Negro for several months when it was without a vicar. In another church a resident Negro minister took several services one summer and he has also preached several times in the winter.

On the other hand, four rectors volunteered the information that the "Negro young people tend to drop out during or after adolescence" and seek out "their own church for social life." Three ministers reported that they believed there would be feeling on the part of their white members against an increasing Negro membership. White church members are reported to have asked: "Why don't they go to colored Episcopal churches?"

All of these forty-three churches in which Negroes are members of some church social organization are located in northern communities. Eighty per cent are in Massachusetts and New York. All of the communities, with the exception of Brooklyn, have small Negro populations. While the degree of integration cannot be reliably described in detail, the situation in the following nine is probably typical:

In Arlington, Mass., a Negro is secretary of the men's group, clerk of the vestry, and a teacher in the Sunday School. While eight Negroes belong to this church, very few attend regularly.

A Brooklyn church with a total membership of 819 has 35 Negro attenders and 90 members. Twenty Negroes are in the women's society which meets in the parish house. Five Negro children are in the Sunday School. Three Negroes are in the young people's society, three are in the choir, and one is a Sunday School teacher. This church is active in the Interracial Fellowship movement.

Five Negroes attend and seven are members in Aurora, New York. One is clerk of the executive committee; two are in the women's society; one is in the choir and secretary of the Altar Guild.

The church board in Ypsilanti, Michigan, has gone on record to extend a "welcome to any colored members of our church." Negroes are said to be welcomed in all organizations except the women's society. There is one Negro family in this church.

Of the three Negroes who attend and six who are members of a Boston church, three are in the women's society, two are in the Altar Guild, and two are in the Sunday School. This congregation "accepted the services of a colored priest when they were without a vicar for several months, but some people ask why don't Negroes go to colored Episcopal churches."

In a Pittsfield, Massachusetts, church there are five colored families. The older Negroes participate in the women's society; the "younger seek out their own church for social life."

A Negro minister who grew up in the parish and who

resides in the community took three services one summer and has preached several times in the winter in a Stoughton, Massachusetts, church. Six Negroes attend regularly and fifteen are members.

In Worcester, Massachusetts, 145 Negroes attend and 100 are members. One is a Sunday School teacher and there are many Negro children in the Sunday School. The young people, however, go to Negro churches for social life. "Some of the other colored people who do not attend this church do not like it and claim Negroes there are trying to gain prestige."

A church in Santa Barbara, California, has four Negro attenders and members. Two are in the young people's society and two are in the choir. This church has one Japanese-American and one American Indian. The latter is on the church board. "One Negro occasionally reads the lesson. . . . Little thought given to race."

Interpretations

While this survey of Protestant churches is not representative of all of the denominations nor of all parts of the country, nevertheless it justifies certain conclusions about racial segregation in the American Protestant Church. It is, of course, overweighted with denominations having a predominantly northern constituency and liberal traditions in race relations. The Congregational Christian churches, for example, are well known for their liberal traditions, both theological and racial, as demonstrated by their participation in the abolition movement, their achievements in the education of Negroes, the work of their Council for Social Action, and the establishment by the American Missionary Association during World War II of a Race Relations Division.[5] Moreover, 27 per cent

---

[5] See Embree, Edwin R., *Brown Americans* (New York: The Viking Press, 1943), pp. 72-87; *Seeking a Way*, Partial reprint of the Biennial Re-

of the Congregational Christian churches are in the New England states, generally assumed to be an area sympathetic to Negroes. No southern denominations are included. Thus no information from 25,000 Southern Baptist churches and 3,500 Southern Presbyterian churches, both noted for their conservative views, is included in this chapter's report. Nor is there any information from the Methodist denomination with approximately 8,000 southern churches.[6] Under these circumstances, the reports just given present Protestantism in the best possible light from the standpoint of how far it has gone in integrating Negroes into the actual life of its local churches.

This is the picture which emerges: There are approximately 8,000,000 Protestant Negroes.[7] About 7,500,000 are in separate Negro denominations. Therefore, from the local church through the regional organizations to the national assemblies over 93 per cent of the Negroes are without association in work and worship with Christians of other races except in interdenominational organizations which involve a few of their leaders. The remaining 500,000 Negro Protestants—about 6 per cent—are in predominantly white denominations, and of these 500,000 Negroes in "white" churches, at least 99 per cent, judging by the surveys of six denominations, are in segregated

port of The American Missionary Association Division of the Board of Home Missions of the Congregational and Christian Churches for 1942-1944; Voss, Carl Hermann, "The Rise of Social Consciousness in the Congregational Churches: 1865-1942," Unpublished Ph.D. Thesis, University of Pittsburgh, 1942.

[6] Dwight W. Culver in an unpublished study of segregation in The Methodist Church estimates that there are about 100 white Methodist churches with Negro participation. These churches have about 100 Negro attenders and 400 Negro members.

Bernard Walton, secretary of Friends General Conference, knows of only seven Negroes among the 17,000 members of Monthly Meetings affiliated with Friends General Conference.

[7] There are approximately 300,000 Negro Catholics in the United States. See Gillard, John T., *Colored Catholics in the United States* (Baltimore: The Josephite Press, 1941), p. 14.

congregations. They are in association with their white denominational brothers only in national assemblies, and, in some denominations, in regional, state, or more local jurisdictional meetings. There remains a handful of Negro members in local "white" churches. How many? Call it one-tenth of one per cent of all the Negro Protestant Christians in the United States—8,000 souls—the figure is probably much too large. Whatever the figure actually is, the number of white and Negro persons who ever gather together for worship under the auspices of Protestant Christianity is almost microscopic. And where interracial worship does occur, it is, for the most part, in communities where there are only a few Negro families and where, therefore, only a few Negro individuals are available to "white" churches.[8]

That is the over-all picture, a picture which hardly reveals the Protestant church as a dynamic agency in the integration of American Negroes into American life. Negro membership appears to be confined to less than one per cent of the local "white" churches, usually churches in

---

[8] A questionnaire addressed to the executive secretaries of approximately sixty city Councils of Churches brought replies from seventeen to a question asking for the number and names of churches in the community having "mixed" membership. Very few "white" churches with more than one racial group were known. While this survey is not conclusive, the information corroborates the results of our survey of 17,900 churches in six denominations. The seventeen cities and the number of churches with more than one racial group were: Oakland, California (one, "interracial church") ; Sacramento, California (o) ; Evansville, Indiana (o) ; Indianapolis, Indiana (one, Episcopal) ; South Bend, Indiana (three, Baha'i, Church of God, Pentecostal Assembly) ; Topeka, Kansas (o) ; Wichita, Kansas (A few churches have Mexicans or Chinese or Indians) ; Flint, Michigan (o) ; Duluth, Minnesota (o) ; St. Paul, Minnesota ("many churches with a *few* Nisei, Chinese, or Negroes"; one Baptist and three Methodist churches named) ; Kansas City, Missouri (o) ; Albany, New York (one, Baptist church has Chinese church school) ; Buffalo, New York (five, names not given) ; Manhattan, New York ("at least a score," no names given) ; Utica, New York (o) ; Cleveland, Ohio (thirty, mostly with Japanese-Americans, a Christian church and a Baptist church mentioned as having Negroes); Portland, Oregon (o) .

small communities where but a few Negroes live and have already experienced a high degree of integration by other community institutions—communities one might add where it is unsound to establish a Negro church since Negroes are in such small numbers. It is an even smaller percentage of white churches in which Negroes are reported to be participating *freely,* or are *integrated.*

The same pattern appears to be true for other colored minorities, that is, Japanese, Chinese, Indians, Mexicans, Puerto Ricans. Regarding the Mexicans and Puerto Ricans, for example, a director of home missions work in a great denomination says his experience leads him to believe that "generally there is little, if any, discrimination here *though in a community which has a large Mexican population it is quite true that they have their own churches."*[9] (Italics mine.)

TRANSITION AREAS

In communities where Negroes live in large numbers and form a substantial portion of the population, they have their own churches. In changing neighborhoods, where Negroes and whites live in the vicinity of a "white" church, Negro attendance and membership is almost invariably resisted. In a few such instances Episcopal churches have encouraged Negro attendance and membership. Usually the gesture is made after most of the white members have moved away and the church, almost overnight, becomes a "Negro" church with a few white members.[10]

---

[9] Personal communication to the author.

[10] There is a Protestant Episcopal church in Philadelphia in an area of Negro infiltration which has Negro and white members and a biracial board. The rector is Negro and there is a part-time white assistant. At present the total membership is 550 (400 Negroes and 150 whites); the average attendance is 225 Negroes and 30 whites. In this particular case, a Negro and a white church combined, the Negro group moving over to the white church. It is significant that no whites are in the young people's society, although all of the other organizations still have a few white members.

The customary pattern in Protestantism is to resist the Negro invasion and then, when transition has occurred, to sell the property to a Negro group. The Episcopalians and the Catholics can meet these situations more gracefully since the equity is not owned by an individual congregation but by a diocese or similar organization which can turn the property over for use as a Negro Episcopal or Catholic church.[11]

This survey of almost 18,000 churches in six denominations has failed to discover a single "white" church with an "open" or mixed membership *in an area undergoing transition*. It is only when colored members are in the majority that membership in transition areas is open.

Sensitive Christians in the white churches—denominational leaders, clergymen and laymen—realize that their moral defenses are down when they do not welcome Negroes into their churches.[12] They know, as do church statisticians, that thousands of white Protestants every year

---

[11] *Memorandum*, An Exploratory Study to Determine the Facts Relative to Neighborhood Change Among Congregational Christian Churches located in communities that have been traditionally white, but which have become or are becoming Negro, and to seek a solution for the problems involved. Mimeographed by the Department of City Work, the Board of Home Missions of the Congregational and Christian Churches, New York City (no date). Signed by Stanley U. North. See also Dorey, Frank, "Community Turnover on the South Side of Chicago; a Study of the Expansion of the Negro Communities and Their Effect on the White Protestant Churches," unpublished B.D. Thesis, Chicago Theological Seminary, 1942. For a discussion of the effects of purchase of churches on race relations see Mays, Benjamin E., and Nicholson, Joseph W., *The Negro's Church* (New York: Institute of Social and Religious Research, 1933), pp. 181ff.

[12] VanKirk, Walter W., *A Christian Global Strategy* (Chicago: Willett, Clark & Company, 1945), pp. 74-81. An excellent survey by a person sensitive to Christian values is found in McCulloch, Margaret C., "Educational Programs for the Improvement of Race Relations: Seven Religious Agencies," *The Journal of Negro Education*, Vol. XIII, No. 3 (Summer Number, 1944), pp. 303-315. Also, Holloway, Vernon H., "Christian Faith and Race Relations," *Religion in Life*, Vol. XIV, No. 3 (Summer, 1945), pp. 1-11. See also Knox, John, *The Christian Church and Race* (in Pamphlet Library on "The Church and Minority Peoples" distributed by the Commission on the Church and Minority Peoples of the Federal Council of the Churches of Christ in America, New York, n.d.).

transfer their memberships from one church to another, not only within a denomination, but from one denomination to another.[13] Negroes do not have this freedom. It is true that there are some *national* minority groups that have separate churches, such as the Swedish or Finnish Congregational Churches. There are also some national minority groups that have separate denominations, such as the Danish Lutherans. While the religious life of these groups may be "segregated," it is not an imposed segregation, because individuals can and do join churches of the same or other denominations. American Negroes, on the other hand, experience an involuntary, imposed type of religious segregation.

Negro migration into white neighborhoods is not a recent problem. The denominations and local churches have largely evaded it. Little study has been given to it. The Congregational Christian Churches through their Board of Home Missions, however, is exploring this situation, with its economic as well as sociological and religious facets. On the basis of information received from the superintendents of thirty-two regional conferences relative to Congregational Christian churches that are in neighborhoods changing from white to Negro, Stanley U. North, Director of the Department of City Work, makes several interesting observations and recommendations:

The answers from the superintendents reflect the baffling nature of the problems involved. . . . Social studies . . . show that the highest incidence of deaths from tuberculosis, juvenile delinquency, houses of prostitution, and murders are in each case to be found in the Negro sections. . . .

The capitalistic aspect of Protestantism is such that those

---

[13] Douglass, H. Paul and Brunner, Edmund deS., *The Protestant Church as a Social Institution* (New York: Harper & Brothers, 1935), p. 54. The authors also cite evidence of the transfer of clergymen from one denomination to another. From one-fifth to one-third of the ministers in some denominations have come from outside the denomination (p. 258).

who are most privileged have the best churches, the finest plants, the ablest leadership, while those who are most needful have the minimum of resources both of plant and staff.

For want of decent housing, adequate schools, sufficient recreational centers and, let it be added, vital and significant religious institutions in its areas of under-privilege, the community pays a terrific price in terms of social waste. . . .

Among the Congregational Christian Churches . . . equities are owned by the local church. Side by side with the worship is the social program. If the leadership attempts to achieve an interracial quality, income in all probability falls off. If the church is of a mind to surrender its plant to a Negro congregation, those white constituents who remain in the neighborhood are inclined to oppose it, believing correctly that such a development will accelerate the Negro invasion. Altruism is conditioned by economics. If the white church is to relocate, it needs to realize the fullest possible amount on its equity. In the very nature of neighborhood change the amount received will be considerably less than replacement costs.

An adequate strategy will not be developed in the realm of theory. There must be experimentation in terms of definite situations with sufficient resources to achieve success if such be possible. . . .[14]

As North says, "side by side with the worship is the social program." Unlike the Catholic Church, worship is rarely the almost exclusive activity of the Protestant Church, though there is evidence that most church-goers attend only the worship service.[15] But even for this group, the service has a different meaning. There is more social interaction and less centering on the altar and its significance. In a recent article, Will W. Alexander summed up the difference between the Catholic and the Protestant churches with reference to the Negro: "The difference is to be found in the fact that, in most cases, a Protestant church is to some extent a social organization as well as a place of worship; the Catholic church, with its emphasis

---

14 *Memorandum,* op. cit., pp. 6-7.
15 Douglass, H. Paul, and Brunner, Edmund deS., *op. cit.,* p. 49.

on worship, is more nearly an altar before which all men are equal."[16]

PRINCIPLES WITHOUT POLICIES

An important factor in the lack of stated racial policies in Protestantism is the structure of the churches themselves. Protestantism is organized in many of its branches on a highly decentralized basis. Even in the Protestant Episcopal, Lutheran, and Methodist communions, there is considerable local church autonomy. Among the Friends, Disciples, and Baptists it would not be exaggerating to say that the political form approaches anarchy. It is little wonder then that respondents to questions on denominational policy with reference to race say that the national bodies at present have no authority over the local church with respect to Negro membership. The Baptists, Congregationalists, Disciples, and Friends emphasize that their general assemblies, conventions, or meetings could not be given any such authority. As one Baptist secretary wrote: "Every church a law."[17]

In all seventeen communions each local church now makes its own policy with respect to admitting Negroes to membership. Among those denominations which by their form of government could adopt a national policy,

---

[16] Alexander, Will W., "Our Conflicting Racial Policies," *Harper's Magazine*, Vol. 190, No. 1136 (January, 1945) , p. 175. Gillard, John T., *op. cit.*, p. 138, says that of the "296,998 colored Catholics in the United States, 189,423, or 63.7 per cent, claim membership in their own churches. The other 107,575 belong to 'white' or 'mixed' churches."

LaFarge, John, *The Race Question and the Negro* (New York: Longmans, Green & Company, 1943) , p. 44, says ". . . there were in the year 1941-42 a total of 306,831 Negro Catholics listed in fifty-nine dioceses of the United States. The number of Catholic Negroes in dioceses not listed was estimated, very uncertainly, at about 10,000. There were 326 Catholic churches for the exclusive use of Negroes, of which there were 15 in the diocese of Baltimore; 36 in that of Lafayette, La.; 26, of Mobile; and 21, of New Orleans." See also John LaFarge, "Caste in the Church: II The Roman Catholic Experience," *Survey Graphic*, Vol. XXXVI, No. 1 (January, 1947) , pp. 61-62, 104-106.

[17] Reply to questionnaire.

it would require, for example, a majority vote of the Protestant Episcopal General Convention, and a majority vote of the General Assemblies of the various Presbyterian bodies subject to final adoption by the local congregations.

But, as we have seen, no stated policies have been adopted by any denomination with regard to Negro membership in local churches. To date all we have are pronouncements. Probably the finest statement is the four principles adopted in October, 1943, by the General Convention of the Protestant Episcopal Church. These four guiding principles had been developed and set forth in more elaborate form by the National Council of the Protestant Episcopal Church in February, 1943. As a general statement they are so far ahead of what the other denominations have announced that we quote them in full.

GUIDING PRINCIPLES DESIGNED TO GOVERN THE CHURCH'S NEGRO WORK
(*As adopted by National Council and approved for publication by Bishop Peabody of the Committee on Reference*)
February 9-11, 1943

It is a first responsibility of the Church to demonstrate within its own fellowship the reality of community as God intends it. It is commissioned to call all men into the Church, into a divine society that transcends all national and racial limitations and divisions. . . . Especially in its own life and worship there can be no place for barriers because of race or color. (1937 Oxford Conference Report.)

We believe that this statement expresses the more Christian basis for judging the prevailing conditions which affect our Negro members and the principles for determining policies and programs for our work involving members of every race. The fact that all these principles cannot be realized at once in their fullness should not prevent us from keeping them before us as the Christian goal.

The four principles stated are:

1. Fellowship is essential to Christian worship. Since there

are no racial distinctions in the mind of the Father, but "all are one in Christ Jesus" we dare not break our Christian fellowship by any attitude or act in the House of God which marks our brethren of other races as unequal or inferior.

2. Fellowship is essential in Church administration. Through the privilege of exercising initiative and responsibility in Church affairs, through fair representation and voting power in all its legislative assemblies, will Negro Churchmen be assured that their fellowship in the Episcopal Church is valid and secure.

3. High standards must be maintained in every department of our work with the Negro. This principle applies to buildings, equipment, maintenance, personnel and general policy in the case of institutions, and especially to training and support of the ministry. Where separate facilities are still maintained, they should provide the same opportunities as those which are available to other racial groups.

4. It is both the function and the task of the Church to set the spiritual and moral goals for society, and to bear witness to their validity by achieving them in her own life. The Church should not only ensure to members of all races full and free participation in worship, she should also stand for fair and just access to educational, social, and health services, and for equal economic opportunity, without compromise, self-consciousness, or apology. In these ways the Church will demonstrate her belief that God "has made of one blood all nations of men for to dwell on the face of the whole earth."[18]

These "Guiding Principles," it must be remembered, were not adopted in this form by the General Convention and they are not a set of directives to local congregations. "But," writes Dr. Almon R. Pepper, executive secretary of the Department of Christian Social Relations, "the National Council's statement on 'Guiding Principles Designed to Govern the Church's Negro Work' is an important statement because it is specific and has to do with the administrative policy of the National Council itself."[19]

---

[18] Single-sheet mimeographed release secured from the National Council of the Protestant Episcopal Church.

This would seem to mean that the "Guiding Principles" are not denominational policies with respect to church membership, but rather, standards for the policies of the National Council itself.

It is interesting to compare the pronouncements of the churches with respect to the forced evacuation of Americans of Japanese descent with their statements on American Negroes. The response of Protestantism to the plight of 130,000 Japanese-Americans was immediate and impressive. The statements and actions of the various bodies were of a very high order, and it is quite evident that some day when the whole story is told, American Protestantism will be found to have played a very constructive role in an otherwise destructive and hysterical action on the part of the United States government.[20] The statements of the churches with regard to the Japanese-Americans provide a sharp contrast with the statements on Negro membership.

In language that could not be misunderstood they called on local churches to welcome the relocated Japanese-Americans.

Northern Baptist Convention, 1944

Resolved, That the churches of our denomination recognize their responsibility to the Americans of Japanese origin as they are resettled in our various communities, and that we welcome them into Christian fellowship of our churches without discrimination.[21]

Church of the Brethren, 1944

We recommend, with respect to Americans of Japanese descent, that our churches welcome into their services and fellowship those who are resettled in their communities. . . .[22]

---

[19] Personal communication to the author.

[20] For a brief account of Protestantism's response see *Beyond Prejudice,* by Toru Matsumoto (New York: Friendship Press, 1946).

[21] *Year Book of the Northern Baptist Convention* (Philadelphia: The American Baptist Publication Society, 1944), p. 275.

[22] *Minutes of the Annual Conference of the Church of the Brethren, 1944* (Elgin, Illinois: Brethren Publishing House), p. 53.

EVANGELICAL AND REFORMED CHURCH, 1944

The General Synod urges the pastors and congregations in communities where these prejudices are still rife, to boldly befriend those against whom these prejudices are directed and help them to find a place in their fellowship.[23]

Other denominations, for instance the Northern Presbyterians, urged their churches "to sponsor one or more of these families, undertaking what is necessary in helping them to become established in a new community."[24]

There does not yet appear to be any sign of the legislative bodies of the churches taking a public stand in favor of an open-door policy with regard to the Negro. On the other hand, there are no barriers in the way of local congregations taking such a position. Within the past few years this issue has been fought out successfully in a church of the Southern Presbyterians in Chapel Hill, North Carolina. Two statements by the church board show how the issue was handled in a church with a relatively liberal constituency and a liberal minister. The officers of this congregation had to work out for themselves a policy since the "Standards of the Church made no direct or indirect reference to the racial problem."[25]

Another possible approach may be through the local councils of churches. It may be too early to evaluate the effectiveness of the "Interracial Code for Protestant

---

[23] *Acts and Proceedings of the Sixth Meeting of the General Synod of the Evangelical and Reformed Church, 1944* (St. Louis: Eden Publishing House) , p. 264.

[24] *Minutes of the General Assembly of the Presbyterian Church in the United States of America, 1944* (Philadelphia: Office of the General Assembly) Part I, p. 233.

[25] While this liberal minister who had welcomed a few Negro students into his church services was sustained by his elders and deacons, according to the minister, as of March, 1946, there are still no Negro members in this church although "Negroes attend the church every now and then without invitation." (Personal communication to the author.) The two statements are "A Consideration of the Church and the Racial Problem by the Elders, March-June, 1944," and "A Consideration of the Church and the Racial Problem by the Elders and Deacons."

Churches" adopted by the Board of Directors of the Detroit Council of Churches on February 17, 1944, but conceivably such codes, if adopted by a large enough number of councils of churches, might not only help the progressive forces in a local church but stimulate the national bodies of some of the denominations. The Detroit Code is worthy of attention because it goes beyond mere platitudinous statement to a number of specifics, including recommendations that the communions affiliated with the Council and the constituent congregations re-examine their interracial practices, welcome Negroes in the churches' neighborhoods into membership, employ and promote individuals on their professional staffs on the basis of ability, regardless of race, and secure qualified representation on boards of control "for any racial group which is consistently represented in the church's membership in its geographical community."[26]

The "Interracial Code," adopted on February 17, 1944, is described in the correspondence columns of the *Christian Century*. After mentioning that the code was carefully drawn by Dr. Alfred McClung Lee, chairman of the department of social service in the council of churches and head of the department of sociology in Wayne University, the correspondent states that it

... was passed by the executive committee without much controversy and with only two opposing votes. But so far as my information goes, not a single church in this city had adopted it. I know of only one church where it has been seriously discussed officially. There are a few eminent ministers of this city, pastors of large and influential churches, who would like to take an advanced position in their churches, even going so far as to make them bi-racial in membership, but none of these ministers have received official encouragement to that end. Or, if so, it hasn't been made public.[27]

---

[26] *Of One Blood All Nations* (Detroit: The Detroit Council of Churches, 1944).

A test of the effectiveness of the "Interracial Code" occurred within a few months after its adoption. The executive secretary of the Detroit Council of Churches recounts the experience of one of the oldest Negro denominations:

> Recently, with the most outstanding leaders of the African Methodist Episcopal Zion Church in the city for a fortnight attending their quadrennial conference, out of fifty "white" churches approached, only one opened its pulpit to any of these distinguished guests, and that for a Sunday evening. Even with such celebrated talent as E. Stanley Jones and Paul Robeson on the program it was found impossible to secure a large "white" church auditorium for a public meeting of what would certainly have been a mixed audience invited to attend the conference.[28]

The "Guiding Principles," the "Chapel Hill" statements, and the Detroit "Interracial Code" demonstrate that the question of Negro membership in white churches is still in the talking stage. Advanced though they are, by their very character they prove that organized Protestantism has no inclusive policy with respect to Negro membership.

SUMMARY

The crux of Protestantism's interracial problem is in the policies and practices of the local churches. National church bodies have little specific information concerning the application of local open-membership policies. A rather

---

[27] Jones, Edgar DeWitt, in "News of the Christian World," *The Christian Century*, Vol. 61, No. 23 (June 7, 1944), p. 705.

[28] Brumbaugh, T. T., " 'The Fault, Dear Brutus,' " *The Christian Century*, Vol. 61, No. 21 (May 24, 1944), p. 644. As of December, 1947, we have learned of no church in Detroit which changed its policy with regard to Negro membership as a result of the "Code."

extensive inquiry made for the purposes of this study shows that the practices of local churches seem to be established by the community situations rather than in response to national policies. Where there is a small Negro population, integration sometimes occurs, and the church reflects it. Where there is a larger Negro population, segregation is the rule and the church reflects that, too. There are a few exceptions and a few rather courageous local experiments which have had, however, little assistance from national church bodies.

CHAPTER 5

What the Churches Do:
In Educational Institutions

Two of the major disabilities of Negroes in the North are occupational and residential segregation; the third is educational segregation.

Denominational institutions, no longer dominant in American education, still have an important place. In the nineteenth century education gradually became accepted as an established function of government; today we have a public system extending from the nursery school through the graduate school. Nevertheless, as recently as 1929-30,

the 278 Protestant colleges and universities provided for about one-fifth of all of our students in higher education. . . . Considering only collegiate departments, the proportion is one-fourth. Reports of enrollments furnished for 1931-32 by thirteen of the major denominations . . . totaled 175,204. In Methodist colleges alone there were 67,490; in Southern Methodist, 29,-282; in Northern Baptist, 28,638; in Presbyterian (U.S.A.), 22,-991; in Disciples, 11,252.[1]

It was said that

the Churches control almost a third of the colleges and universities of the country, own one-fourth of the properties involved, and furnish one-third of the endowment. In number of teachers employed in proportion to enrollment, and expenditure per student, these institutions compare favorably with others.[2]

---

[1] Hartshorne, Hugh, Stearns, Helen R., and Uphaus, Willard E., *Standards and Trends in Religious Education* (New Haven: Yale University Press, 1933) , pp. 132-133.

Private education still plays a significant role despite depressions and competition from state universities. Some of the weaker denominational colleges have gone out of business, but in 1944 one could find classified as white institutions controlled by Protestant denominations 251 four-year colleges and universities and 101 junior colleges.[3]

WHAT IS A DENOMINATIONAL COLLEGE?

For the purposes of this report the foregoing statistics require several qualifications. We surveyed only non-Negro higher educational institutions controlled by fifteen denominations in the Federal Council of Churches, the Southern Baptists, the Friends General Conference, and the other Friends Yearly Meetings (see list on page 147). Furthermore, a large number of Protestant institutions are in the South where separate schools for white and Negro students are maintained. Our examination of racial policies is confined to institutions *not* located in the following states where public schools must be separate: Alabama, Arkansas, Delaware, Florida, Georgia, Kentucky, Louisiana, Maryland, Mississippi, Missouri, North Carolina, Oklahoma, South Carolina, Tennessee, Texas, Virginia, West Virginia, and also the District of Columbia.[4]

---

[2] Hartshorne, Hugh, Stearns, Helen R., and Uphaus, Willard E., *op. cit.*, p. 217.

[3] U. S. Office of Education, *Educational Directory, 1944-45* (Washington, D. C.: United States Government Printing Office, 1944), p. 7. The discrepancy between our figures and those cited in *Standards and Trends in Religious Education* is to be found in the matter of definition. Our statistics are based on the data furnished the Office of Education which requests institutions applying for admission to listing in the *Educational Directory* to state the *legal* control under which the institution operates. The number of colleges *affiliated* with a denomination is, of course, much larger.

[4] ". . . all public schools must be separate and pupils of the white and Negro races are not permitted to attend the same school." Mangum, Charles S., Jr., *The Legal Status of the Negro* (Chapel Hill: The University of North Carolina Press, 1940), p. 79. (The Maryland law is treated

The problem of separating denominational and unde-
nominational private colleges is difficult.[5] There are several sources which list "denominational" institutions.[6] We
chose to use the roster of institutions of higher education
outside of the South described in the *Educational Directory, 1944-45* of the United States Office of Education as
being under the control of the seventeen Protestant denominations. This method reduces the number of institutions, but since this is a study of the policies and practices of the denominations themselves, it seems the fairest
procedure.[7]

---

by Mangum on page 80.) Mangum states on p. 104: "Separate higher
educational facilities are maintained in all of the southern and border
states, even where the prohibition against mixed schools is statutory and
not constitutional." According to Mangum only four states, Florida, Kentucky, Oklahoma, and Tennessee, expressly require that private education
be separate. See p. 103.

[5] See Charters, W. W., "The Denominational College," *Association of
American Colleges Bulletin*, Vol. XXXI, No. 2 (May, 1945), p. 296-298, for
a thoughtful analysis of how to define a denominational college.

[6] For example, Wickey, Gould and Anderson, Ruth E., eds., *Christian
Higher Education*, (Fourth Edition of the *Christian Education Handbook*)
(Washington, D. C.: Council of Church Boards of Education, 1940); Landis, Benson Y., *op. cit.*, pp. 118-130; U. S. Office of Education, *Educational
Directory, 1944-45* (Washington, D. C.: United States Government Printing Office, 1944). (The last volume has the smallest number of denominational institutions of all sources consulted.) In addition, each denomination
has an agency which publishes lists of "its" educational institutions.

[7] A post card was mailed with a covering letter to the heads of ninety-
eight colleges and universities, requesting information on the number of
students of racial minorities (American Indians, Chinese Americans, Japanese Americans, Mexican Americans, Negro Americans, others) enrolled
in 1939-44 and in 1944-45. Each institution was also asked the number of
colored Americans on its faculty or board and its present policy on admitting colored Americans. Seventy replies were received. (65 co-educational,
four for men, one for women.)

Institutions surveyed and their replies are listed in Appendix III A. In
Appendix III B is a brief report of a supplementary survey of 15 church-
related colleges located in these border states: Maryland, Missouri, West
Virginia, and the District of Columbia. In recent years a few colleges and
seminaries in these states have been enrolling Negroes, so the Protestant
colleges were questioned to find out the trend of their policies and practices. The border state institutions are not treated in the text.

NEGROES IN NORTHERN DENOMINATIONAL COLLEGES

Thirty-two colleges for the five-year period, 1939 to 1944, had 165 students. Almost one-half of the sixty-two colleges (30) that provided information had not a single Negro. Only ten colleges had as many as five or more Negro students, that is, an average of at least one in each year.[8] See Table III.

TABLE III

NEGRO ENROLLMENT IN 62 CHURCH-CONTROLLED COLLEGES, 1939-44

NUMBER OF COLLEGES	NUMBER OF NEGRO STUDENTS	TOTAL
30	0	0
9	1	9
7	2	14
4	3	12
2	4	8
1	5	5
1	6	6
2	7	14
1	8	8
1	11	11
1	13	13
1	15	15
1	20	20
1	30	30

In 1944-45 a majority of these colleges (36) still were without Negro students.[9] Only ten colleges enrolled three or more Negro students. Eighty-one Negro students, in all, were enrolled in that year. Since the total enrollment in the seventy colleges in 1944-45 was approximately 22,000, the proportion of Negro students was about 0.36 per cent. See Table IV.

---

[8] Eight colleges have not been included in this summary because even though the writer interpreted their replies as meaning no Negro students in 1939-44, one could not be certain that no Negro students were enrolled during the period.

[9] The replies of three colleges for 1944-45 have also been excluded, because they were ambiguous.

TABLE IV

NEGRO ENROLLMENT IN 66 CHURCH-CONTROLLED
COLLEGES, 1944-45

NUMBER OF COLLEGES	NUMBER OF NEGRO STUDENTS	TOTAL
36	0	0
15	1	15
5	2	10
3	3	9
2	4	8
1	6	6
1	7	7
1	8	8
2	9	18

It is doubtful if the other colleges and universities that did not reply, also classified by the Office of Education as under denominational control, differ markedly in the number of Negro students enrolled. This judgment is based on the surveys made annually by *The Crisis* of Negroes enrolled in or graduating from American colleges.[10] Only four Protestant colleges not replying to our questionnaire (Butler University, University of Denver, Drew University, and Hamline University) appear in *The Crisis'* list of northern and western institutions.

The Crisis data for the academic years 1939-40 through 1944-45 not only substantiate the judgment made about the colleges which did not answer our inquiries, but also contrast the enrollment of Negro students in public and private colleges and universities with their admission by denominationally controlled institutions.

An inspection of the figures published in *The Crisis* shows that the large majority of Negro students who attend northern institutions go to the state universities. A small group goes to the well-known private (non-church) universities. There is a sprinkling in some of the small non-

---

[10] See the August issues of *The Crisis* for the annual survey.

denominational colleges and, as our survey confirms, an insignificant number of Negro students in the church-controlled colleges.

THE NATIONAL SURVEY OF THE HIGHER EDUCATION OF NEGROES

The planners of an exhaustive study of higher education of Negroes proceeded on the apparently well established assumption that the vast majority of Negroes who attend northern institutions are enrolled in either public universities or a few of the outstanding non-denominational private universities. Thus, they chose Kansas, Illinois, Ohio State, and Cincinnati among the public universities, and Chicago, Northwestern, New York University, and Teachers College of Columbia University from the non-denominational private universities. Some remarkable findings that have a direct bearing on the role of Protestant colleges in the integration of Negro Americans came out of this study, the most noteworthy from both an economic and sociological point of view being that "whereas very few southern Negroes were attending these eight northern universities in 1939-40, in the year preceding, nearly 4,000 northern Negroes attended Negro colleges. Almost 3,000 of this number attended colleges in Southern States."[11]

There were 635 Negro students in the four public universities and 618 in the four private universities. Seventy-seven per cent were residents of the state in which the institution was located and only 14 per cent came from the South and of the 88 students from the South, 63 were graduate students.[12]

---

[11] Caliver, Ambrose, *National Survey of the Higher Education of Negroes —A Summary* (Washington: U. S. Government Printing Office, 1943), Misc. No. 6, Vol. IV, p. 13.

[12] U. S. Office of Education, *National Survey of the Higher Education of Negroes: General Studies of Colleges for Negroes* (Washington: U. S. Government Printing Office, 1942), Misc. No. 6, Vol. II, p. 79.

Seventy per cent of the 1,253 students in these eight universities had attended mixed high schools, indicating that the "majority of the students, therefore, had been residents of northern cities at least since early adolescence."[13] These Negro students, on the whole, were well prepared to meet the universities' standards. They had a

... median percentile ranking which exceeded the median for the total student body in Ohio State University (55.5). The Negro students fell slightly below the median at the University of Chicago (47.5) and considerably lower at the University of Kansas (23.9). The medians in the reading tests were similar to those of the psychological examinations. In grade-point averages for five universities, the Negro students had a median grade of C, with a normal distribution in the various grade intervals at each institution.[14]

THE PROTESTANT COLLEGE'S ROLE

The denominational colleges in the North, with a few exceptions, have not even begun to grapple with this problem which has vital implications for the present and future welfare of Negro Americans, and, we would emphasize, for Americans of all complexions. This is demonstrated with especial poignancy for three northern states:

... Kansas, Ohio, and Pennsylvania, in which Negro colleges were located, together had 1,722 Negro residents attending Negro colleges in 1938-39. Of this number, 718 students attended Negro colleges within their own states, while forty-eight went to one of the Negro colleges in another northern state. The remaining 946 students resident in these states attended Negro colleges in southern states.[15]

"Thus in 1938-39, the Negro colleges of the southern states provided educational facilities for 946 residents of

---

[13] Caliver, Ambrose, *op. cit.*, p. 13.

[14] *Ibid.*, p. 13.

[15] U. S. Office of Education, *National Survey of the Higher Education of Negroes: General Studies of Colleges for Negroes* (Washington: U. S. Government Printing Office, 1942), Misc. No. 6, Vol. II, p. 83.

these three northern states, while in the same year all the southern states together sent to the four Negro colleges in these three states only 218 students."[16]

The data we have assembled make it possible to examine the contribution of the Protestant colleges in Kansas, Ohio, and Pennsylvania.

The eight church-controlled "white" colleges in Kansas enrolled for the five-year period 1939-44 fifty-two Negro students. In 1944-45 there were ten Negro students enrolled. In Ohio, of the twelve Protestant colleges, the seven replying to our inquiry enrolled approximately thirty-six Negroes during 1939-44; in 1944-45 nine colleges enrolled twenty-two. In Pennsylvania eleven of the eighteen church institutions enrolled eight Negro students during the five-year period 1939-44, and in 1944-45 nine colleges said they had six.

Thus twenty-six colleges in these three states had ninety-six Negroes over a five-year period—less than one Negro per college per year. In 1944-45, twenty-six colleges had thirty-eight Negro students, an average of approximately one and one-half Negro students per college. Contrast these figures with the 946 Negro residents of these states who went to southern Negro colleges.

Pennsylvania, with the second largest Negro population of any state outside of the South, 470,172 in 1940, has eighteen Protestant church-controlled colleges and universities and six church-related institutions. On the basis of the present survey and information secured from informed sources, the writer believes that these twenty-four institutions in 1944-45 did not have ten Negro students.

No Negro was regularly on the teaching staff or board of any denominationally controlled college.[17]

---

[16] *Ibid.*, p. 83.
[17] The survey was made in the spring of 1945. Since that time a few institutions have appointed Negro professors. See Haygood, William C.,

SECONDARY SCHOOLS, JUNIOR COLLEGES,
AND SEMINARIES

Church secondary schools are difficult to define. The Office of Education compiles no data on denominational control, and Porter Sargent's well-known *Handbook of Private Schools* does not in every case clearly distinguish between church relatedness and church control. However, the Sargent *Handbook* and information supplied by denominational headquarters yielded a satisfactory list of 134 Protestant schools not located in the South. Eighty-one of them are related to the Episcopal Church; the Friends have twenty-nine; the remaining twenty-four are divided among five other denominations.

The available information about Negro enrollment in these schools is, unfortunately, quite incomplete. Reports from fifty-six of them show that during the five-year period, 1939 to 1944, only two schools had Negroes enrolled (six Negroes were in one school, one in the other). For the 1944-45 school year, only two of these schools had Negroes enrolled (one school had four and the other had one).[18]

No school replied that a Negro was on its faculty or board of trustees. (See Appendix III D.)

Only eleven junior colleges outside of the South, according to the *Educational Directory, 1944-45*, are under the control of Protestant churches. From five of them came information that in two institutions a total of nine Negro students had been enrolled in the five-year period, 1939 to 1944; in 1944-45 one junior college had three Negro students.[19]

"Negro Teachers in White Institutions," *Phi Delta Kappan*, Vol. XXVIII, No. 2, (October, 1946), pp. 74-75, for a listing of Negroes who have taught in white institutions during the past few years. See also Wale, Fred G., "Chosen for Ability," *Atlantic Monthly*, Vol. 180, No. 1, (July, 1947), pp. 81-85.

[18] Since 1945 a few of these schools have admitted Negro students.
[19] See Appendix III C.

No Negro was on the faculties or boards of trustees.

Thirty-nine non-southern theological seminaries are classified by the *Educational Directory, 1944-45,* as under the control of our seventeen denominations. Information from thirty of them shows seventy-eight Negro students in the period, 1939 to 1944.[20] Twelve seminaries of the thirty did not have any Negroes enrolled at all in this five-year span.

TABLE V

NEGRO ENROLLMENT IN 30 CHURCH-CONTROLLED SEMINARIES, 1939-44

NUMBER OF SEMINARIES	NUMBER OF NEGRO STUDENTS	TOTAL
12	0	0
6	1	6
1	2	2
4	3	12
1	6	6
1	7	7
2	8	16
2	9	18
1	11	11

In 1944-45 thirteen seminaries reported thirty-eight Negro students. Seventeen reported none.

TABLE VI

NEGRO ENROLLMENT IN 30 CHURCH-CONTROLLED SEMINARIES, 1944-45

NUMBER OF SEMINARIES	NUMBER OF NEGRO STUDENTS	TOTAL
17	0	0
5	1	5
1	2	2
3	3	9
1	4	4
1	5	5
1	6	6
1	7	7

[20] For both periods, 1939-44 and 1944-45, a few seminaries' replies could not be understood and have not been included in the text. The doubtful replies are indicated by a question mark in Appendix III E.

Almost every seminary, however, insisted that Negroes were admitted on the same basis as other applicants.

None of these church-controlled institutions had a regularly appointed Negro on its faculty. Nor did any of these institutions have a Negro on its board of trustees. During 1944 Howard Thurman of Howard University taught at Berkeley Baptist Divinity School while he was co-pastor of an interracial church in Berkeley.

WANTED: DENOMINATIONAL POLICIES

In general, then, we find that the Protestant educational institutions enroll Negroes in negligible numbers and that their practices are almost the counterpart of congregational practice. Like the local church, a few institutions have one or two Negroes; like the local church, no aggressive campaign is being undertaken to admit Negroes, to encourage Negroes to apply for admission, or to develop a sense of community in which Negroes will "feel at home."

Denominational conventions, again as in the case of congregational membership, have made some rather general pronouncements with regard to the enrollment of Negroes in their colleges, but again, as in regard to local churches, they have adopted no explicit racial policies. The Disciples of Christ in 1934 recommended that Negro divinity students be admitted to their "white" colleges. The Northern Presbyterians in 1943 recommended that ". . . our Colleges . . . work toward the goal of making available their privileges, activities, ministry, and fellowship equally to all races. . . ."[21] In 1946 and 1947 the following denominations made reference to the racial practices of their educational institutions: Church of the Brethren, Congregational Christian, Evangelical and Reformed, Presbyterian U.S.A., and United Presbyterian.

---

21 *Minutes of the General Assembly of the Presbyterian Church in the United States of America, 1943* (Philadelphia: Office of the General Assembly) Part I, p. 201.

In spite of the fact that no denomination has any policy with regard to its colleges admitting Negroes, there seems to be no good reason why this has to be so. It is true, of course, that only rarely do national church bodies elect members to the boards of trustees of the colleges. More often it is a state or regional body that exercises this authority, and in many cases the college board of trustees is permitted to choose its own members provided they are members of the church. But this remoteness of control need not be a barrier to effective policies in the matter. Nearly all of the denominations have boards that attempt to develop closer relationships between the colleges and the churches. The degree of church board control is not at all uniform. There is a strong movement within the denominations to strengthen the relationship between the churches and the colleges. Thus the Northern Presbyterians have announced:

1. The college shall adopt a statement of purpose clearly defining the status as a Christian college . . .
2. It shall be the declared policy of the college to employ as regular members of the faculty only men and women who are active members in good standing of some evangelical Christian church which affirms its loyalty to Jesus Christ as the Divine Lord and Savior. The Board does not rule that this action is to affect faculty members already employed.
3. The college shall provide courses in biblical studies and shall require at least one such course for graduation. . . .[22]

The Northern Baptists and the Methodists who, with the Presbyterians U.S.A., have more colleges than other denominations, are also attempting to strengthen their ties

[22] From *Set of Standards* for colleges affiliated with the Presbyterian Church, adopted by the Board of Christian Education, Presbyterian Church, U.S.A., April 28, 1943, and approved by the General Assembly. *Minutes of the General Assembly of the Presbyterian Church in the United States of America, 1944* (Philadelphia: Office of the General Assembly) Part II, p. 84.

with the colleges. Even the Congregationalists, famed for their decentralization of control, are now renewing denominational bonds.

These closer ties should surely make it possible for "pronouncements" to be turned into effective policies opening the way to an increase in Negro enrollment in denominational colleges.

Voluntary and Involuntary Segregation

We have seen how in 1938-39 almost three thousand northern Negro students attended segregated institutions in the South while only 165 Negro students for a five-year period, 1939-44, were enrolled in 62 northern church-controlled colleges. Could any evidence be stronger of Protestantism's failure to contribute to the integration of Negroes into American life?

The National Survey of the Higher Education of Negroes indicates that it is unlikely that Negro students in the near future will rush to enter the church colleges even if the church colleges should make it widely known that Negro students will be considered on the same basis as white students:

> Negro students were found to face a number of special problems in northern institutions, primarily in terms of finances, housing, and the lack of participation in campus life. Negro students seldom lived on the campus and, in general, they seemed not to "belong" in the same way that white students feel themselves a part of the university.[23]

---

[23] Caliver, Ambrose, *op. cit.*, p. 13. The questions raised by Caliver as to "why . . . such large numbers of Negroes go South to attend Negro colleges . . ." could be studied with profit by Northern college administrators and faculties. See especially pp. 13-14. College administrators might also consider the recommendation by the President's Committee on Civil Rights for state fair educational practice laws even though the Committee said that "educational institutions supported by churches and definitely identified as denominational should be exempted." See *To Secure These Rights* (Simon and Schuster, 1947), p. 168.

As far as the denominational colleges are concerned, not until the administration and faculty as well as the student body and townspeople learn how to treat "colored" people as people will the increasing voluntary segregation of Negroes, typified by the nearly three thousand northern Negro students attending southern colleges, begin to decrease. This is more easily said than done. A thorough educational program will be required in most institutions before Negro students can participate freely in *all* the campus activities. Once such changes in attitudes have occurred on a college campus, the college might indicate that Negro students are welcome by appointing Negroes to its faculty and its board of trustees, establishing special scholarships, and assisting its Negro graduates to find employment.[24]

Protestant colleges need not think that opening their doors to Negro students is an act of charity. These colleges are failing to be intelligent about the ignorance of white students and their responsibilities to the building of understanding among America's racial groups. As Donald Young says, "We should do well to heed Moton's shrewd observation":[25]

The white man's knowledge of Negro life is diminishing, and the rate is accelerated by the present-day policy of segregation. This operates practically to make an ever widening gulf between the two races. which leaves each race more and more ignorant of the other. Without contact there cannot be knowledge: segregation reduces the contacts, and so knowledge and understanding decrease. With the decreasing knowledge come increasing distrust and suspicion, and these in turn engender prejudice and even hatred. So a vicious circle is established whose ultimate effect, unless counteracted, must be a separation

---

[24] See "No One Group, a statement about the beliefs and work of the Race Relations Committee at Antioch College, Ohio, 1945."

[25] Young, Donald, *American Minority Peoples* (New York: Harper & Brothers, 1932) , p. 497, quoting Moton, R. R., *What the Negro Thinks* (Garden City, N. Y.: Doubleday, Doran & Company, Inc., 1928) , p. 5.

of the races into more or less opposing camps, with results as disastrous to the spirit of American institutions as to the genuine progress of both races.

The bugaboo of "intermarriage" will have to be faced, since, as Young says:

Racial intermarriage is a threat which drives white Americans wild. If two races go to school together, it is violently stated miscegenation, legal or illicit, must increase. There are plenty of contacts outside of the school between the sexes of different races to allow more than sufficient opportunity for a maximum of race crossing. There are powerful social forces at work in every state of the Union which will continue to restrict marital eligibility in accordance with group conventions, and this means that interracial marriages will remain in a forbidden category whether or not the children are segregated in school. Not every classmate is a potential husband or wife for the American girl or boy even in white schools. There is no noticeably greater amount of sexual relationship of any sort between colored and white people in those northern communities where all children attend the same school than where they are divided by race; and it may even be that there is less than in the South where, in spite of educational segregation, *ante bellum* traditions and the presence of an under-privileged caste encourage miscegenation, contrary to legal and other policies.[26]

Douglass and Brunner in their discussion of Church colleges observe: "The original primary purpose of all these institutions was to inculcate religion and train religious leaders; and all still officially endeavor to produce an educational climate favorable to religion."[27] One might ask whether any college can have an "educational climate favorable to religion" unless every group in American society is in its student body, urban and rural, rich and poor, Jew and Gentile, Negro and white.

---

[26] Young, Donald, *op. cit.*, p. 472.
[27] Douglass, H. Paul and Brunner, Edmund deS., *op. cit.*, p. 166.

SUMMARY

The pattern of racial segregation that prevails among Protestant churches is found among Protestant educational institutions as well. National Protestant church bodies have done little to change the situation beyond issuing "pronouncements" from time to time. Effective policies are lacking. The role of the Christian college is such as to give it a special responsibility to renounce segregation and create an educational "climate" in which all races share.

CHAPTER 6

Toward Racial Integration

WE BEGAN this book with the sobering assertion that Protestantism, by its policies and practices, far from helping to integrate the Negro in American life, is actually contributing to the isolation of Negro Americans. We have in the intervening chapters presented our evidence. Some important things remain to be said.

Today, as never before, Negroes are alert and sensitive to the slightest discrimination—the working class as well as the "talented tenth." The evidence is overwhelming, we believe, that Protestantism by the example of its churches and its educational institutions is sanctioning the status quo; and it is the status quo that Negro Americans resent. The Protestant Church is in danger of becoming in the eyes of millions of Americans, if it is not already, the symbol of the philosophy of white supremacy.[1] Nowhere is this truer than in the South; but the pattern of segregation is rarely disturbed in the North, even among the most liberal denominations. The church is not only following the community patterns of segregation; in many instances, as we have seen with respect to its schools and colleges, the church is lagging behind the local customs. Its practices actually help to perpetuate the system of segregation.

To be sure, one has to make exceptions. There are clergy-

---

[1] See the analysis of the Protestant vote in 1944 presidential election by John C. Bennett of Union Theological Seminary in "Correspondence," *The Christian Century*, Vol. 61, No. 50 (December 13, 1944) , p. 1450. See also the biting comments on "the society of the white Protestant élite" in "The Talk of the Town," *New Yorker*, Vol. 21, No. 10 (April 21, 1945) , p. 17.

men and laymen who feel acutely the contradictions between the Christian ideals and the practices of the church
and its members. Many youth groups, in every denomination, have expressed a growing impatience with the in-
difference and inertia of their churches. Students at many
colleges have been agitating that their administrations
admit Negroes.[2] In many communities the youth and the
women's organizations, notably, the United Council of
Church Women, are less apt to set themselves off racially
than are the ministers.

THE PATTERN OF SEGREGATION

If the churches should announce a policy of racial in-
clusiveness, it would be a challenge to the larger society.
It would be a symbol to all, if done with conviction. But
the churches will have to overcome the formidable obstacle
of social stratification. The same process that causes
wealthy whites to attend one church and the poor whites
another operates even more powerfully to keep the races
apart. Even "the Roman Catholic Church includes parishes
especially for Negroes, Italians, Poles, French Canadians,
Germans, Irish and others."[3] Race is just one more factor

---

[2] Student opinion also revealed itself to be more in tune with what
Myrdal calls the American creed in the placement of relocated Japanese-
American students. There is a significant indication of the attitudes of
many youth in the *Message of Friendship from the Young Friends* at
Friends' General Conference, 1944. Friends very rarely issue pronouncements, and yet in the case of the statement drawn up by 250 members
of their high school section the Friends' General Conference had the
message printed for distribution.

[3] Young, Donald, *American Minority Peoples* (New York: Harper &
Brothers, 1932), p. 510. Myrdal and his associates agree with this, at least
so far as Negroes are concerned. "On the whole, the Roman Catholic
Church prefers to have Negroes attend all-Negro churches, on the basis of
residential segregation and attempts to dissuade them from attending
white churches." Myrdal, Gunnar, *An American Dilemma* (New York:
Harper & Brothers, 1944) II, p. 870. Summing up the findings of the
various studies by his associates of the smaller sects, Myrdal says: "The
Holiness Church, while predominantly white, has occasionally bi-racial
congregations," "a small number of upper class Negroes" have joined the

to add to the complexity of factors that go to make up class consciousness. Color has become so important and so influential that many social scientists in an effort to interpret race relations in American society have turned to the concept of caste as the term most nearly describing Negro-white relationships.[4]

Social stratification is usually accompanied by residential segregation. Since the Protestant Church with its multiplicity of sects and denominations has had, until the coming of modern transportation, a neighborhood membership, we find another factor strengthening the exclusive character of the average congregation. Negroes, living on the "other side of the tracks" or in some other area to which they are restricted temporarily or permanently by custom, social pressure, or restrictive covenant, would be unlikely to visit, let alone be invited to attend, the white man's church.

The former executive secretary of the Detroit Council of Churches shows the intimate relationship between residential segregation, restrictive covenants, and "ecclesiastical exclusiveness" in one typical northern city with a large Negro population. In writing of the need for additional housing, he said:

. . . Yet every proposed site for such projects brings protests from certain interests that "existent patterns" are threatened, even though these *interests* are a mile or more distant. Progress is blocked. For a need of as many as 20,000 houses for Negro

---

white-dominated small Bahai Church and that perhaps 10 per cent of the Father Divine Peace Mission movement is white. Myrdal, Gunnar, *op. cit.*, p. 871.

[4] Davis, Allison and Dollard, John, *Children of Bondage* (Washington, D. C.: American Youth Commission of the American Council on Education, 1940) ; Dollard, John, *Caste and Class in a Southern Town* (New Haven: Yale University Press, 1937) ; Myrdal, Gunnar, *op. cit.;* Warner, W. L., Junker, B. H., and Adams, W. A., *Color and Human Nature* (Washington, D. C.: American Youth Commission of American Council on Education, 1941) .

occupancy, the secretary of the Detroit Housing Commission reported recently that only "a few hundred" are under construction.

Restrictive covenants are a device of the privileged classes of society to maintain that which they cannot otherwise preserve. It is of these classes also that the most influential of our old-line American churches are composed. It is in this manner, therefore, that practices and policies of segregation came to obtain in our churches. For even though at the lower levels of economic and cultural stratification there may be no such color line and citizens work, play, ride and shop together without regard for such differences, most American congregations are affiliated with denominations whose policies are determined by elements desiring such segregation. Hence our almost exclusively "white" and "colored" congregations even within the same Protestant denominations throughout America.

Detroit is probably Exhibit A among northern cities in such ecclesiastical exclusiveness. The writer knows of only one "reputable" church in the city where Negroes have membership with whites and there they are so few as to justify rather than discredit such generalization. It is not at all uncommon to hear of churches where Negro children have been asked to withdraw from "white" Sunday Schools, and more than one Woodward avenue church has felt obliged to decline the use of its facilities for Negro or mixed gatherings. . . . [5]

Thus, some of the immediate practical effects of Protestant exclusiveness in maintaining segregation are seen in housing and education. Without implying that Protestantism alone is responsible for the injustices and discriminations experienced by Negroes, certainly the church must be held partly accountable, by its sins of omission and commission, for the Negro's inferior status in other areas such as employment, health, civil rights, housing, and education. But at bottom the Protestant Church has probably done the greatest injury to Negro Americans in sanctioning the status quo by the example of its all-white congregations.

---

[5] Brumbaugh, T. T., *op. cit.*, p. 644.

An "Impossible Ideal"?

The churches' practices in the United States are apparently having repercussions abroad. Alexander points out that Protestantism has had high hopes for an expanded missionary program in Asia and Africa, but he warns the churches that the peoples of these continents are increasingly suspicious of Christianity as it is practiced by white Americans. He wonders if Protestantism can carry its message abroad with much prospect of success as long as Negro and white Christians worship separately.[6]

As Pearl Buck and Gunnar Myrdal, to mention but two students of America's racial patterns, have been saying, America's moral leadership in world affairs is bound up with her treatment of her colored minority peoples.[7] America's greatest barrier to moral leadership, thinks Myrdal, is her treatment of the Negro. In Asia especially, Japan has given tremendous publicity to our shortcomings. For its international prestige, power, and security, the United States must prove to the world that its Negroes can be made part of its democracy.[8]

Myrdal says the Negro problem is not only America's greatest failure, but also her greatest opportunity. He says that America has always stood for equality, freedom, and liberty. If America can show that justice, equality, and co-operation are possible between the white and black races, Myrdal believes that

... America's prestige and power abroad would rise immensely. The century-old dream of American patriots, that America should give to the entire world its own freedoms and its own faith, would come true.

---

[6] Alexander, W. W., "Our Conflicting Racial Policies," *Harpers Magazine*, Vol. 190, No. 1136 (January, 1945), pp. 178-179.

[7] Buck, Pearl S., *American Unity and Asia* (New York: The John Day Company, 1942); Myrdal, Gunnar, *op. cit.*

[8] Myrdal, Gunnar, II, *op. cit.*, pp. 1015-1021.

... And America would have a spiritual power many times stronger than all her financial and military resources—the power of the trust and support of all good people on earth.[9]

Is the organized church a "tremendous resource for interracial reform"? Those who would answer in the affirmative might profit by the note of realism sounded by Arthur L. Swift, Jr., sociologist and professor at Union Theological Seminary:

I do not believe that American Christians are as a rule victims of divine discontent over their racial prejudices. I doubt they are in any large numbers keenly aware of this American dilemma.

. . we must not allow the urgency of the issue to cloud our judgment. What likelihood is there that organized religion can make significant contribution in the field of race relations? Let us first consider its inevitable limitations. It is integrally a part of the social structure it should strive to change, profiting by the very injustices against which it should protest, guilty of the crimes it should condemn, in despite of its Godward vision a very human agency indeed. . . . The church should be in moral and ethical advance of slow-moving majorities. It should lead the way. But if we mean by "the church" the members of organized religious groups they constitute fifty-five per cent of our population—a majority which cannot be in advance of itself. And in somewhat the same fashion the church has become one with our social and economic structure. As long ago as 1926 it was estimated that its capital investments totaled more than seven billions of dollars. It has a tremendous stake in the *status quo.* . . . As constituted it is not an instrument ideally adapted to the production of social change. Yet it has now and then nurtured and then promptly denounced some major prophet of righteousness. And by preaching, if not by example, it has held before men's eyes the noble, "impossible" ideals of justice and brotherhood, building and sustaining that moral tension between high desire and low attainment, which keeps us divinely dissatisfied.[10]

---

[9] *Ibid., pp.* 1021, 1022.

[10] Swift, Arthur L., Jr., "The Church and the American Creed," *Friends Intelligencer,* Vol. 103, No. 7 (February 16, 1946) , p. 100. See also Niebuhr,

GOOD WILL PLUS

In our time can we do more than *hope* for a "non-segregated Church and a non-segregated society"? As we look ahead and attempt to estimate the forces making for integration, we can point to many favorable changes in the race relations climate. In many parts of the United States the spade work has been done and the seeds planted. And the seeds have taken root.

In public education, industry, social work, and government the pattern of segregation is under attack. In some parts of the country integrationists have the offensive; witness intercultural movements in schools, state fair employment practices legislation, the popularity of books dealing with intergroup relations.

It is too soon to know how deeply American attitudes have been changed. Perhaps this whole movement for interracial justice and fellowship is only a fad to be swept aside for some other cause. For despite the many favorable changes in public sentiment supporting interracial justice and fellowship, optimism has to be restrained as one considers the tense pattern of international relations and the threat of depression. What would happen to Negro workers in a depression?

And what will happen to Negroes in the event of war or threat of war? A precedent for dealing with a racial minority in time of war has already been set by the United States government: 100,000 Japanese, a majority American born, were uprooted from their homes and businesses and thrown into "relocation camps."

But barring war and depression, and given a continuation of the present movement for racial justice and fellow-

H. Richard, *The Social Sources of Denominationalism* (New York: Henry Holt and Company, 1929), pp. 236-263; Myrdal, Gunnar, *op. cit.*, II, pp. 858-878; Johnson, Guion G. and Johnson, Guy B., "The Church and the Race Problem in the United States," unpublished MS, Schomburg Collection, New York Public Library, n.d.

ship, the church has an opportunity such as it may never have again.

Thousands of church people, professional and laymen, young and old, men and women, are participating in the interracial movement. This story, which runs from discussion of the race problem and exchange of pulpits, through active participation and leadership in community projects, to bold experimentation with interracial churches, ought to be told.[11] Many, many churchmen today have a real concern and are acting.

The Congregationalists, for example, have made 1946-48 a period for church-wide emphasis in race relations. The biennium committee and staff were offered the following program of specific procedures:

A.   Inquire into current policies and practices of our denominational agencies and our church-related colleges and schools to discover any segregation or discrimination which may exist, that it may be replaced by inclusive policies and practices.

B.   Assist local churches in examining the widespread practices of restriction and racial exclusiveness in membership, attendance, fellowship in worship and social activities, church administration, staff employment, and ministry, that these may be replaced by inclusive and non-discriminatory policies and practices.

---

11 See Johnson, Charles S. and Associates, *Into the Main Stream,* (Chapel Hill: University of North Carolina Press, 1947) especially pp. 281-333, for an account of some "best practices in race relations in the South." See also the "Resource Manual in Christian Intercultural Relations," mimeographed by Committee on Church and Race, 287 Fourth Avenue, New York. For "The Emergence of the Interracial Church" see Homer A. Jack's article under that title in *Social Action,* Vol. XIII, No. 1 (January, 1947) pp. 31-38.

In many organizations, local, state, and national, white Protestant men and women have been the leaders in interracial activities. In a few denominations there are extensive programs in the field of group relations. There is a need for a careful summary and evaluation of the role of white Protestants as leaders and supporters of programs for interracial justice and fellowship.

C. Aid local churches and church members in developing a sense of moral and religious responsibility for, and skill in overcoming, discriminatory social and economic customs and practices in their communities—for example, restrictive housing covenants, differential employment practices, unequal administration of the law, inequitable and segregated use of community facilities and public services.

D. Enable local churches and church members to develop abilities to co-operate with non-church agencies and persons as well as with other local church forces in achieving more nearly inclusive patterns of community life.

E. Encourage the development of standards of human relations such as the "Intercultural Code" prepared by the Intercultural Committee of the Council for Social Action.

F. Promote participation by representatives of local churches in the annual Institute of Race Relations at Fisk University and in other camps and conferences inclusive in character.

G. Develop opportunities for persons of diverse ancestries to work together in a variety of projects of common interest, and to meet together for study and discussion of human relations.

H. Stimulate the use of literature, drama, audio-visual aids, and graded educational materials in the program of emphasis.

I. Plan the strategy and program of the denomination in these fields both to meet immediate emergencies and crises and to take account of long term regional, national, and world trends.

J. Broaden and increase the giving of our church people through the Postwar Emergency Program for these objectives.[12]

Unfortunately, most of the action by churchmen and non-churchmen, in view of the present state of our knowledge of human relations, is of a trial and error character. Rather than list another set of "Things to Do," we would

---

[12] *Minutes, Eighth Regular Meeting, General Council of the Congregational Christian Churches of the United States* (New York: 1946), p. 47.

call the attention of church leaders to a neglected approach.[13]

Needed: A Study of Experiments

We have in mind the need for social research to accompany social action. There is an extraordinary amount of experimentation going on. Some of it appears to be successful. But we will never be certain as to why certain projects and programs succeed or fail until we apply the scientific method.

While the methods and achievements of social science lag far behind physical science, no longer need we be apologetic about its value. World War II demonstrated the worth of social science to the Armed Services. The Department of Agriculture for many years has found social science a good investment. Lately industry has been employing social psychologists, anthropologists, and sociologists to bring to bear on problems of human relations the knowledge and methods slowly accumulated by social scientists.

The church, too, might take advantage of what social science has to offer. Denominational headquarters might well collaborate with research groups or add to their staffs trained social scientists to put their skills to work on the most effective methods of implementing denominational pronouncements.[14] Considering the fact that only the Congregational Christian Churches have adopted an explicit program to remove "the sins of caste," this proposal may seem premature. However, the Federal Council of

---

13 Some excellent suggestions for churches and churchmen are made in Liston Pope's article, "A Check List of Procedures for Racial Integration," *Social Action*, Vol. XIII, No. 1 (January, 1947), pp. 38 to 43.

14 ". . . Social-action programs are still in the embryonic stage in all but a few denominations. Denominational grants for social-action departments are meager, personnel inadequate and a trained social leadership lacking." Judson T. Landis, "Social Action in American Protestant Churches," *American Journal of Sociology*, Vol. LII, No. 6 (May, 1947), p. 517. (abstract).

Churches has adopted a forthright set of principles on integration and several members have concurred. Social research could assist these bodies to implement their pronouncements.[15]

SPECIFIC PROBLEMS FOR STUDY

At least three situations facing the "white" Protestant denominations call for social research:

First, many denominations have no Negro members. What methods might be used to add Negroes to these bodies?

Second, hundreds of "white" churches in metropolitan areas are being surrounded by Negro populations. There is no tested body of knowledge to present to the leaders of these churches as to what alternatives are possible and what are the costs and consequences.

Third, scattered throughout the North and West are several hundred congregations where two or more racial groups are worshipping together. These churches could be laboratories for social research. What are the conditions that make possible integration in the church? Some of the answers might be found by research conducted under one denomination or a joint project through the Federal Council of Churches.

More than goodwill is needed. More than pronouncements. Yes, and as important as explicit positive policies are, more than policies. Tested techniques are also needed to guide men and women of good will.

Men need to hear the call of prophetic voices. They need to be reminded of their selfishness and self-complacency. They need to have the goals of brotherhood and

15 For descriptions of some recent "action-research" see David Krech (editor), "Action and Research: A Challenge." *Journal of Social Issues,* November, 1946, Vol. 2, No. 4 and Lippitt, R. and Radke, M., "New Trends in the Investigation of Prejudice," *The Annals,* March, 1946, pp. 167-176.

justice proclaimed by their churches. But they also need to be shown how to achieve the goal of integration. When the church states certain ends to be good, it has a moral obligation to try to find the means. Social research is one method of finding the means of building "a non-segregated Church and non-segregated society."

SUMMARY

If one were to write a history of Protestantism's relations to Negroes the balance sheet would be heavily on the debit side. Protestantism arose in the time of European exploitation of non-white peoples. It blessed slavery.[16] It sanctioned a caste system with its stamp of inferiority on a whole race. But there were exceptions. Individuals and some groups became sensitive to the incompatibility of the Christian ethic and the slave system. Some dedicated their lives to teaching the freedmen.[17]

Latterly this number of concerned individuals has grown and we find many church members devotedly working for "a non-segregated Church and a non-segregated society." Although Protestantism, by its policies and practices is still actually contributing to the segregation of Negro Americans, there is some ground for confidence that the intelligence and devotion of these pioneers will show a way. Let us hope that it may come sooner than we think.

---

[16] Tannenbaum, Frank, *Slave and Citizen* (New York: Alfred A. Knopf, 1947).

[17] Brownlee, Fred L., *New Day Ascending* (Boston: The Pilgrim Press, 1946).

APPENDIXES

Appendix I

PRONOUNCEMENTS CONCERNING NEGROES

A. ABSTRACTS OF PRONOUNCEMENTS, 1908 TO 1929[1]

FEDERAL COUNCIL OF CHURCHES, 1919

Negroes should be fully recognized as American and fellow citizens, given equal economic and professional opportunities, increasing participation in all community affairs; a spirit of friendship and co-operation should obtain between the white and colored people, North and South. They should have parks, playgrounds, equal wages for equal work, adequate schools, equal facilities and courtesy when traveling, adequate housing, lighting and sanitation, police protection, and equality before the law. Especially should the barbarism of lynching be condemned by public opinion and abolished by vigorous measures and penalties.

FEDERAL COUNCIL OF CHURCHES, 1924

The assumption of inherent racial superiority by dominant groups around the world is neither supported by science nor justified by ethics. The effort to adjust race relations upon that basis and by the use of force is a denial of Christian principles. To demonstrate that Christian ideas are sufficient to solve the difficult problems of race relations in America is the supreme domestic task before the churches today.

BAPTIST, NORTHERN CONVENTION, 1922

All good citizens, North and South, deplore lawlessness in the form of lynching and mob violence in the treatment of Negroes and all unchristian acts as well as illegal discrimination of race against race. Legislation is needed to remedy these conditions. Much can be accomplished by interracial conferences.

STATEMENT, SOUTHERN BAPTIST CONVENTION, 1929

Affirms unalterable opposition to mob violence in all forms and belief in the enforcement of all law and the impartial administration of justice and the regular and orderly process of the courts against all offenders of whatever race, class or station.

---

[1] Compiled and summarized by Johnson, F. Ernest, ed., *The Social Work of the Churches.* (New York: Department of Research and Education of the Federal Council of the Churches of Christ in America, 1930) , pp. 154-155.

CONGREGATIONAL CHURCHES, 1919, 1923

Our people should exert their influence against intolerance on account of race, color, nationality, or creed.

CONGREGATIONAL CHURCHES, 1925

The American principle should be put into practice of giving the same protection and rights to all races who share our common life. Racial discrimination should be eliminated and there should be substituted full brotherly treatment for all races. There should be the fullest co-operation between the churches of various races though of different denominations.

METHODIST EPISCOPAL, SOUTH, 1928

Christ's teachings concerning human brotherhood demand equal justice and opportunity for all persons regardless of race, color or sex.

PROTESTANT EPISCOPAL, 1919, 1922

Mob violence in every form is wrong; it is a clearly defined and imperative Christian duty to sustain the civil authorities in the righteous exercise of their powers in seeing that even-handed justice is unfailingly administered according to due and lawful process.

FRIENDS GENERAL CONFERENCE, 1927

Friends General Conference rarely issues pronouncements. The following statement has been used by almost all of the Yearly Meetings which are members of Friends General Conference:

We recognize it to be our duty as Christians to inform ourselves regarding those of other races and nationalities within our own country . . . that we may be qualified to exert our influence in establishing a high standard of individual and national conduct toward them. Friends should rise above prejudice and unjust discrimination in dealing with persons of other races and in speaking of them . . . as individuals. . . .

Above all, while other races either within or without our borders remain in economic, mental, or spiritual bondage, we cannot be true to the obligation which our common brotherhood imposes upon us without doing our utmost to remove the burden from them and to give them assistance and co-operation in obtaining an opportunity equal to our own.[2]

---

[2] *The Book of Discipline of the Religious Society of Friends,* adopted by Philadelphia Yearly Meeting, Fifteenth and Race Streets, 1927.

B. Analysis of Pronouncements, 1930 to 1939[3]

The following phrases are literal or equivalent renditions of passages in pronouncements made by various denominations in the years shown.

1. All races same protection and rights: N. Baptist, 1935; Brethren, 1935; Cong. Christian, 1934, 1938; Disciples, 1937; Evangelical and Reformed, 1932; Methodist Episcopal, 1932.

2. All men opportunity to develop, fulfill duties, and enjoy privileges as members of families, workers, citizens: Methodist Episcopal, 1939; Methodist Episcopal South, 1939.

3. Mutual goodwill and cooperation among races: Evangelical and Reformed, 1932; Methodist Episcopal South, 1934; Pres. U.S., 1936; Pres. U.S.A., 1934, 1937, 1939; Federal Council, 1932.

4. Condemn flogging and lynching. Call on Church members to arouse public opinion: Brethren, 1935; Cong. Christian, 1934; Disciples, 1936, 1937; Pres. U.S., 1936; Pres. U.S.A., 1936; Prot. Episcopal, 1934.

5. Endorse Costigan-Wagner bill: Cong. Christian, No Date; Five Years Friends, 1935; Pres. U.S.A., 1936, 1937; Federal Council, 1933.

6. Endorse Wagner-Van Nuys bill: Disciples, 1937.

7. Urge approval of Cavigan Anti-Lynching bill: Reformed, 1937.

8. Lynching should be a federal crime: N. Baptist, 1935; Cong. Christian, 1934; Pres. U.S.A., 1937, 1939; Federal Council, 1934.

9. Protest to federal and state authorities against laxity of law enforcement: Brethren, 1935.

10. Conferences: no discrimination: N. Baptist, 1935; Cong. Christian, 1931*; Disciples, 1934; Federal Council, 1931.

11. Urge our churches and leaders to voice convictions of justice for all in Scottsboro case: Cong. Christian, 1934; Pres. U.S.A., 1937, 1939; Federal Council, 1933.

---

[3] The statements have been condensed from *Social Pronouncements, 1930-1939* (Chicago: The International Council of Religious Education, n.d.), pp. 15-17. There are no pronouncements dealing with the Negro on the part of the Evangelical Church, The United Lutheran Church, The United Presbyterian Church. Nor are there any pronouncements for Friends General Conference, which is not a member of the International Council. The pronouncements of the Southern Baptist Convention, also not a member of the Council, have been separately compiled and abbreviated by the author. See Numbers 28 and 29 on page 124.

* —without approval or disapproval.

12. Negro should get jury trial by peers; no exclusion because of color: Cong. Christian, 1934; Pres. U.S.A., 1937.
13. Our churches should make a thorough study of race problems in our communities: Disciples, 1934; Pres. U.S., 1936.
14. Not satisfied with condemnation of discrimination but shall cultivate proper attitude toward and between races: Evangelical and Reformed, 1935; United Brethren, 1933.
15. Endorse achieving greater awareness of discrimination through preaching, study groups, and literature: Disciples, 1932.
16. Commend Race Relations Sunday: Pres. U.S.A., 1939; Reformed, 1934.
17. Commend Ass'n Southern Women Opposed to Lynching: Pres. U.S.A., 1937; Federal Council, 1933.
18. Commend Brotherhood Week: Pres. U.S.A., 1939.
19. Opposed to all forced segregation: N. Baptist, 1935, 1939; Cong. Christian, 1934.
20. Dedicate selves to work for equal opportunity for Negro: N. Baptist, 1939.
21. Recommend that our graduate schools offer equal opportunity for Negro ministerial training: Disciples, 1934.
22. Urge convention with Negro Disciples: Disciples, 1934.
23. Favor inviting races within our Church to summer schools, camps, and local church meetings: E. and R., 1932.
24. Commend work of Interracial Commission: Pres. U.S.A., 1937.
25. Each race has distinctive cultural contribution to humanity: Brethren, 1935.
26. Where states fail to guarantee fair trial, federal government obligated to act: Pres. U.S.A., 1938.
27. Condemn every discriminatory law, anti-racial organization, unfair tactics of labor or capital: N. Baptist, 1939.

.   .   .   .

28. We condemn lynching and all forms of lawlessness; pledge our support of all public officials in their efforts for the enforcement of the law: Southern Baptist Convention,[4] 1930, 1931, 1933, 1934, 1935, 1936, 1937, 1939.
29. We pledge ourselves to give our efforts to the correction of many inequalities and injustices which still exist, such as the distribution of school funds, administration of justice, wages paid for Negro labor: Southern Baptist Convention,[4] 1939.

---

[4] Compiled and abbreviated by the author; for this reason, quotations are not indicated. For the complete statements see *Annual of the Southern Baptist Convention* for each given year.

C. Analysis of Pronouncements, 1940 to 1944[5]

For 1940 to 1947 there is no summary in any one source of the pronouncements of all the denominations. Since most denominations have not compiled their pronouncements, the statements for this period usually can be secured only by going through the convention proceedings of each denomination.

One should remember that some denominations have general meetings annually, for example, the Northern Baptists, the Brethren, the Disciples, the three Presbyterian bodies and the Reformed Church in America. The Congregational Christian Churches and the United Lutherans and the Evangelical and Reformed Church meet biennially. The Protestant Episcopal Church meets triennially. The Evangelical Church, The Methodist Church, and the United Brethren have quadrennial meetings and, of course, the Five Years Meeting of Friends convenes every five years. The Southern Baptists meet annually and Friends General Conference biennially. The volume of production of pronouncements may not be unrelated to the number of meetings.

FAIR EMPLOYMENT PRACTICES LEGISLATION

1. Endorse principles of Fair Employment Practices Committee which we hope will be made permanent by act of Congress: Congregational Christian, 1944; Evangelical and Reformed, 1944; Presbyterian U.S.A., 1944; Federal Council of Churches, 1944.
2. Endorse principles of the Fair Employment Practices Committee; urge all agencies involved in administration of the act to improve that administration: Methodist, 1944.

EQUALITY OF OPPORTUNITY

1. Protest against denial of equal employment opportunities: Evangelical and Reformed, 1942.
2. Seek to remove every discriminatory practice, law, anti-racial organization and unfair tactics of capital or any other movement that inflicts injustice upon any group, race, creed, or political affiliation: Northern Baptist, 1940, 1941.
3. Churches, industries and government should be impartial in granting liberty and opportunity to all: Northern Baptist, 1942.

---

[5] We have tried to preserve the original wording wherever possible, but because we have had to abbreviate the voluminous statements in this compilation in order to conserve space, quotations are not indicated.

4. Equal opportunity in employment, up-grading, and conditions of work, full rights of citizenship; in housing, transportation, educational facilities: Northern Baptist, 1944; Methodist, 1944; Federal Council, 1942.
5. Advocate right of every person to equality of opportunity: Protestant Episcopal, 1943.
6. Protest against social, economic, or political discrimination based on race: United Brethren, 1941.
7. Believe that the right of all men to pursue work of their own choosing and to enjoy security from want and oppression is not limited by race, color, or creed: (From "Guiding Principles for a Just and Durable Peace") Federal Council of Churches, 1942.
8. All men regardless of race, creed, class or nationality shall have access to economic means of well-being: Disciples, 1942.
9. Oppose discrimination in opportunities for employment in, and training for, the defense industries: Presbyterian U.S.A., 1941, 1942; Federal Council of Churches, 1941, 1942.
10. Commend government, industry and labor for progress made in removing barriers from war industries: United Presbyterian, 1943.

TRANSPORTATION

1. Rejoice in Supreme Court decision guaranteeing Negroes equal traveling accommodations: Presbyterian U.S.A., 1941.

SEGREGATION

1. Injustices growing out of segregation and discrimination in housing, employment, schools and churches call for program to bring justice to all racial groups: Northern Baptist, 1944.
2. Shall work for elimination of segregation and economic and social discrimination: Evangelical and Reformed, 1944; Presbyterian U.S.A., 1944.

POSTWAR SETTLEMENT

1. Recommend United Nations commitment to principle of racial equality: Methodist, 1944; Presbyterian U.S.A., 1943.

RACISM

1. Opposed to all claims of racial superiority. Our common life has been enriched by contributions from many racial groups: Evangelical, 1942; Evangelical and Reformed, 1942; Presbyterian U.S.A., 1940.

2. Condemn as anti-Christian all activities and attitudes that endanger distrust, suspicion, and exploitation among the races of the world and the minority groups in our own land: Evangelical and Reformed, 1944.

3. Shall work for a social order in which national, religious, and racial prejudice will be non-existent and each race and nationality permitted free development of its native genius: Evangelical and Reformed, 1944.

4. The Christian citizen will combat racial prejudice against Negroes, Anti-Semitism, and unsympathetic treatment of Japanese in internment areas: Presbyterian U.S., 1943.

BLOOD SEGREGATION

1. Deplore segregation of blood plasma: Northern Baptist, 1942.

ARMED SERVICES

1. Oppose discrimination against the Negro in the military services: Presbyterian U.S.A., 1941, 1942; Federal Council of Churches, 1942.

2. Commend War and Navy Departments upon steps taken toward removing discrimination and segregation of Negroes in the Armed Forces, and hope that where practicable all such barriers will be removed: Presbyterian U.S.A., 1944.

3. Commend government for progress in removing barriers from military service: United Presbyterian, 1943.

POLL TAX

1. Urge abolition of poll tax: Congregational Christian, 1944; Evangelical and Reformed, 1944; Presbyterian U.S.A., 1941, 1943, 1944.

2. Recommend study and appropriate action concerning legislation such as Senate 1280: Presbyterian U.S.A., 1942.

CIVIL LIBERTIES

1. Support governmental authorities in protecting civil liberties of all races, political, and religious groups: Northern Baptist, 1940; Evangelical and Reformed, 1944.

2. All children shall have unrestricted privilege of attaining full rights of citizenship: Congregational Christian, 1942.

3. Stand for recognition of rights of the Negro: Methodist, 1944.

4. Equal rights and complete justice for all men in all stations of life: Methodist, 1944.

5. Justice for all races in the administration of the law: Presbyterian U.S.A., 1944.

LYNCHING

1. Rejoice that sacrifice of human life by mob violence has practically disappeared and urge diligence that this form of barbarism may be banished: Southern Baptist, 1940, 1941.
2. Deplore fact that Federal anti-lynching legislation still awaits enactment: Evangelical and Reformed, 1944; Presbyterian U.S.A., 1941.
3. Equal protection through agencies of law and order: Methodist, 1944.
4. Recommend study and appropriate action concerning legislation putting the authority and resources of the Federal Government against lynching, such as House of Representatives 971: Presbyterian U.S.A., 1942.

GENERAL

1. Rejoice in continual lessening of racial antipathies and increase in racial understanding: Southern Baptist, 1940.
2. Shall strive to cultivate interracial good will so that members of Negro race shall have impartial justice, better and more equitable opportunities in industrial, business, and professional engagements, more equitable share in public funds, more adequate opportunities in education: Southern Baptist, 1940, 1941, 1944.
3. Reaffirm our deep and abiding interest in welfare of all races, particularly the Negro race: Southern Baptist, 1941, 1944.
4. We must deal with the race problem of our land on a different principle, according to which differences will not be permitted to generate bitterness and justice will have a human and Christian, rather than a racial, criterion: Southern Baptists, 1943.
5. We seek a *modus operandi* that will diminish friction, eliminate injustices, and promote friendly co-operation: Southern Baptist, 1943.
6. Christianity must not be identified with any one race: Brethren, 1940.
7. Commend Brethren Service Committee for administering relief regardless of racial affiliations: Brethren, 1943.
8. Express concern for the common person . . . who is a soul of eternal worth regardless of race or nationality: Brethren, 1943.
9. Regard with sorrow and alarm antagonism directed against Jews, Negroes, Mexicans and American Japanese: Brethren, 1944.

10. The Church must put forth a special effort to improve class, race and color relationships in the world: Evangelical, 1942.
11. Stand for the rights of racial groups: Methodist, 1940, 1944.
12. Will use every opportunity for manifesting towards different races and nationals a Christian spirit and seek for them fair treatment and fine opportunities of life and development: Presbyterian U.S., 1943.
13. Decent, intelligent Negroes today are entitled to own or rent clean and comfortable homes and to lead their lives in a pure, moral atmosphere: Presbyterian U.S., 1944.
ι. Not satisfied with condemnation of racial discrimination but shall cultivate proper attitudes towards and relations between racial groups: United Brethren, 1941.
15. Urge a more sincere effort to manifest the Christlike spirit to alien and minority groups: United Presbyterian, 1943, 1944.
16. Believe a true Christlike spirit will do much toward removing racial discrimination, especially in industry: United Presbyterian, 1944.

EDUCATION AND ACTION IN THE LOCAL CHURCH

1. Urge our people to search out causes of racial antipathies: Brethren, 1944.
2. Study more deeply problem of creating and maintaining peaceful human relationships in our communities: Brethren, 1944.
3. Appeal to each State Conference, local association, and church to study own community and to work toward co-operative, interracial solutions to problems of its area: Congregational Christian, 1944.
4. Urge our churches to support and to use race relations programs and facilities of following groups: American Missionary Association, Council for Social Action, and Federal Council of Churches: Congregational Christian, 1944.
5. Urge our churches to support Race Relations Sunday, Brotherhood Week, and other opportunities for united religious fellowship: Congregational Christian, 1944; Presbyterian U.S.A., 1944.
6. Ministers and laymen urged to take initiative in setting up interracial groups: Evangelical and Reformed, 1944.
7. Suggest that General Synod invite as fraternal delegate a Negro clergyman from community in which General Synod happens to meet: Evangelical and Reformed, 1944.
8. New social service and missionary ventures should be under-

taken on the basis of interracial co-operation: Evangelical and Reformed, 1944.

9. Recommend Social Creed to be read to congregations once a year or placed in their hands in printed form: Methodist, 1940, 1944.

10. Recommend in every local Church a committee to encourage study and application of Social Creed: Methodist, 1940, 1944.

11. Through conferences, literature, church school, laymen's groups, the Church should seek to discover the mind of Christ in race relations: Methodist, 1944.

12. Urge in our schools and colleges special courses and activities promoting racial understanding: Methodist, 1944.

13. Minister and lay leaders should seek to encourage within the official leadership of local church a Christian attitude toward situations requiring racial understanding and good will: Methodist, 1944.

14. Representatives of both racial groups should pray, study, work together to discover and interpret issues in conflict situations: Methodist, 1944.

15. Through General Conferences, Annual Conferences, and similar meetings, the church should make its corporate influence felt against the evils of racism. It should seek to have interracial commissions appointed in nation, state, and every community where racial groups are to be found: Methodist, 1944.

16. Christians should practice justice and fairness to all races: Presbyterian U.S.A., 1944.

17. Urge Churches and Church groups to assist Negroes to gain full opportunities for education, employment, upgrading, and vocational training: Presbyterian U.S.A., 1944.

18. Urge Churches to use Executive Order 8802 as a standard in evaluating practice of management, labor unions, educational authorities and public officials: Presbyterian U.S.A., 1944.

19. Urge our members to re-examine their own attitude toward the Jew, Negro, Oriental, Indian, and Mexican; their own tolerance of injustice and estrangement between their own groups and racial or religious minorities: Presbyterian U.S.A., 1944.

20. Urge our churches to foster in their communities the spirit that puts first our oneness as children of God, surmounting differences between Jew and gentile, black and white, Occidental and Oriental, foreign- and American-born: Presbyterian U.S.A., 1944.

21. Urge upon our Churches freedom from social prejudice as a vital

qualification for leaders or teachers in any Christian educational program: Presbyterian U.S.A., 1944.

DENOMINATIONAL CONVENTIONS AND ASSEMBLIES

1. Commend Committee on Arrangements of 1944 convention in securing privileges of racial equality at headquarters hotel: Disciples of Christ, 1944.
2. Recommend that committees arranging for general meetings of the church locate such meetings only in places where adequate and suitable entertainment can be provided for all delegates and representatives: Methodist, 1944.
3. Committee on Arrangements shall strive to make arrangements that will allow colored delegates and visitors to be accorded the same treatment as white delegates: Protestant Episcopal, 1940.
4. Recommend that every commissioner regardless of race or color be accorded full rights and privileges of the Assembly: Presbyterian U.S.A., 1943.

COLLEGES

1. Recommend that our colleges make available their privileges, activities, ministry, and fellowship equally to all races: Presbyterian U.S.A., 1943.
2. Urge upon our colleges freedom from racial prejudice as a vital qualification for leaders or teachers: Presbyterian U.S.A., 1944.

ECCLESIASTICAL STRUCTURE

1. Hope that all synods and presbyteries will become racially inclusive: Presbyterian U.S.A., 1944.
2. Look to ultimate elimination of racial discrimination within the Methodist Church and ask Council of Bishops to create forthwith a commission to consider afresh the relations of all races included in the membership of the Methodist Church and to report to the General Conference of 1948:   Methodist, 1944.

FELLOWSHIP IN THE CHURCH

1. Dedicate ourselves and seek to commit our churches to teaching, preaching and full practice of Christian relationships with all people, that we seek every possible way of enlarging our fellowship without discrimination: Northern Baptist, 1944.
2. Unalterably opposed to the segregation of the Negro race, a policy all too often practiced by the Church itself. Participation

and membership in the activities of our Churches must be open to Negroes: Evangelical and Reformed, 1944.

3. We recommend that the churches confess in penitence the contradiction between the profession and the practice of brotherhood within their own Church life, that they prayerfully and earnestly seek to overcome this fault; that to this end our local churches work toward the goal of making available their privileges, activities, ministry, and fellowship equally to all races: Presbyterian U.S.A., 1943.

4. Fellowship is essential to Christian worship.
Fellowship is essential to Church administration.
High standards must be maintained in every department of our work with the Negro; and
It is both the function and the task of the Church to set the spiritual and moral goals for society, and to bear witness to their validity by achieving them in her own life: Protestant Episcopal, 1943.

5. If our communities are to be led into a fellowship like the Kingdom of God, that Fellowship should continue to grow in our churches. Racial discrimination against Negroes and other minority groups has persisted in our communities partly because it has not been eliminated from our churches: Federal Council of Churches, 1942.

.   .   .   .

No pronouncements concerning Negroes were adopted during 1940 to 1944 by the Reformed Church in America, United Lutheran Church in America, Religious Society of Friends (Five Years Meeting) or Friends General Conference.

D. ABSTRACTS OF PRONOUNCEMENTS, 1945 TO 1947[6]

SEGREGATION IN THE CHURCH

1. We affirm as our own these words adopted by the Federal Council of Churches of Christ in America (meeting at Columbus, Ohio, March 5-7, 1946):

    The Federal Council of Churches of Christ in America hereby renounces the pattern of segregation in race relations as unnecessary and undesirable and a violation of the Gospel of love

---

[6] The sources are the minutes of the denominational meetings.

and human brotherhood. Having taken this action, the Federal Council requests its constituent communions to do likewise. As proof of their sincerity in this renunciation they will work for a non-segregated Church and a non-segregated society: Congregational Christian, 1946; Disciples of Christ, 1946, 1947; Evangelical and Reformed, 1947; Presbyterian U.S.A., 1946, 1947.

2. Call upon synods, presbyteries, local churches to renounce the principle of segregation: Presbyterian U.S.A., 1946; (reaffirmed 47).

3. Encourage congregations which lie within, or adjacent to, communities which include racial groups other than the majority group, to recognize their responsibility to minister to the entire community, including persons of other races. Pastors should be encouraged to take the initiative in launching a program looking toward an unsegregated church in an unsegregated society: Evangelical and Reformed, 1947.

4. Believe that racial segregation in society, and even more in the church, is contrary to the letter of the New Testament and to the spirit of the Christian faith. We commend those who are now promoting brotherhood. Congregations have conducted schools of race relations. Our people have welcomed members of other races into the fellowship of our schools, our churches, our camps, and our homes. We would urge our people to abound more and more along these lines: Brethren, 1947.

5. Recommend that our Churches welcome people of all races into their services and full fellowship: United Presbyterian, 1946, 1947.

6. Recommend that the General Assembly, Synod, Presbyteries, and churches of our denomination take unequivocal stand against segregation in any form in any area, refusing to accept accommodations for meeting, eating or sleeping which in any way discriminate against members of these groups on account of race or color, and standing at all times for the principle of equality of all men, whether this be in situations of racial tension, questions of residential restrictions, or problems of opportunity for minority peoples in economic, social and political life: United Presbyterian, 1947.

7. Urge the Synods involved to redefine the boundaries of Presbyteries to accord with principle of non-segregation: United Presbyterian, 1947.

8. Request the appointment of a Biracial committee for the pur-

pose of developing plans to stimulate increased participation of Negro laymen in the established program of the Church: Protestant Episcopal, 1946.

9. Instruct the Assembly's Committee to explore the possibility of setting up a separate Presbyterian Church for Negroes with the present congregations of the Assembly, of the Presbyterian Church, U.S.A., and of the United Presbyterian Church, with a generous place in our budget for its support: Presbyterian U.S., 1946.

10. Now is the time for our Church not only to declare her position on race relations but to demonstrate brotherhood by making possible interracial fellowship: Evangelical, 1945.

11. Our Discipline well says, "The church respects human personality inherent in the people of every race, and protests against social, economic, or political discrimination based merely on racial differences." We therefore, urge all our members:
   1. To encourage interracial fellowship.
   2. To maintain friendly relations through the home, school, and church.
   3. To oppose all practices of racial segregation.
   4. To help open our churches to men of all races.
   5. To support legislation in harmony with these convictions.
                        Evangelical United Brethren Church, 1946.

DENOMINATIONAL INSTITUTIONS

1. Call upon seminaries and colleges and other church agencies and bodies to renounce the principle of segregation: Presbyterian U.S.A., 1946.

2. Encourage denominational Boards and church-related institutions, especially colleges and hospitals, to examine their past and present practices to detect and correct any deliberate or unconscious discrimination against members of any minority groups among students, patients, staff, or administrative Boards: Evangelical and Reformed, 1947.

3. Recommend that provision be made for the Board of American Missions to establish scholarships at all United Presbyterian colleges for members of minority racial groups as a means of acquainting our youth with these Christians of other races: United Presbyterian, 1947.

4. Recommend that the Board of Christian Education provide for scholarships to summer youth conferences for young people of

various racial strains for the encouragement of social and spiritual cooperation on the part of our church leaders of the future: United Presbyterian, 1947.

FAIR EMPLOYMENT PRACTICES LEGISLATION

1. Commend the adoption by New York of a State Fair Employment Practices Act: Presbyterian U.S.A., 1945.

2. Urge Federal action on Fair Employment Practices legislation: Presbyterian U.S.A., 1945, 1947.

3. Urge several states and/or Congress to pass legislation providing for a Permanent Fair Employment Practices Commission with enforcement powers: Northern Baptist, 1946.

4. Commend New York and New Jersey in setting up anti-discrimination laws for employment: Reformed Church in America, 1945.

5. Urge the enactment of Fair Employment Practices legislation by state legislatures and serious consideration by the Congress of the United States: Northern Baptist, 1947.

6. Petition the President of the United States and the Chairmen of interested Congressional Committees to use all the resources of their high offices to influence and bring about the immediate consideration by Congress of the legislation now pending as S. No. 101 and H.R. No. 2232 designed to set up a permanent governmental agency to break down racial and religious discrimination in private and government industry and employment: Congregational Christian, 1946.

7. Approve legislation to secure fair employment practices and to guarantee full human rights to minority groups in our country: Evangelical, 1945; Evangelical and Reformed, 1947.

RACIAL RESTRICTIVE COVENANTS

1. Oppose restrictive covenant agreements with regard to the purchase of real estate and homes in the local community: Northern Baptist, 1946; Congregational Christian, 1946;* Evangelical and Reformed, 1947; United Presbyterian, 1947.

HATE GROUPS

1. Call upon its members who belong to organizations still practicing racial discrimination to work for the elimination of such

---

* The General Council recommended that the committee responsible for the biennial program consider restrictive covenants.

practices, and urge them to refrain from association with all groups that exist primarily for the purpose of fomenting strife and division on the basis of difference of race, religion and culture: Presbyterian U.S.A., 1946.

PRESS AND RADIO

1. Commend Press and Radio for objective way in which they, with few exceptions, present news, editorial and entertainment programs so as to emphasize human qualities rather than racial differences: Presbyterian U.S.A., 1947.

POLL TAX

1. Commend the adoption by Georgia of anti-poll tax legislation: Presbyterian U.S.A., 1945.
2. We must support federal legislation abolishing poll tax: Northern Baptist, 1946; Evangelical, 1945; Presbyterian U.S.A., 1947.

LYNCHING

1. Condemn lynching and devices which deprive minorities of civil rights: Evangelical, 1945; Evangelical and Reformed, 1947; Presbyterian U.S.A., 1947.
2. Commend church organizations of Georgia that have condemned lynching and that have demanded legal action: Federal Council of Churches, 1946.

CIVIL LIBERTIES

1. Condemn all organizations and individuals in our country whose aim and purpose is to hinder any American minorities in the exercise of their civil rights, or that seek to deny such rights to any groups or individuals because of their race, creed, class or color.

   That since our American Congress has seen fit to maintain its Committee on Un-American Activities, the Assembly call upon this Committee to be no less concerned to investigate and expose Un-Americanism of organizations like the Columbians and the Ku Klux Klan—which are definitely akin to fascism—than to expose organizations whose subversive activities stem from their communist character.

   Urge all our people to be on guard in their own communities against all possible violations of the civil rights of their fellow citizens, and that wherever possible they throw their influence and the influence of their local churches on the side of those forces that seek to uphold for all kinds of, and classes of Americans their civil and constitutional liberties: Presbyterian U.S., 1947.

2. We believe in democracy according to which equal political rights are granted to all citizens on a common basis of qualification. The exclusive rule of one race in multiracial democracy, without regard to the right of races to participate in the processes of self-government under a common law, is no more justifiable than the rule of one political party without regard to the rights of other political parties to participation in the processes of self-government under a common law: Southern Baptist, 1947.

EQUAL OPPORTUNITY

1. In Education—That in educational opportunities provided for out of public funds Negro children and white children shall share equally in proportion to their numbers.

In Citizenship—That the constitutional rights of Negroes as American citizens to participate in the political life of the community, state and nation be respected.

In Economic Employment—That Negroes shall have equal opportunity for employment in keeping with the talents, training, and experience of the individual at a wage to be determined by the character of the service rendered.

In National Services—That the right and duty of Negroes to serve in all branches of government service and of the armed forces of the nation, according to the talents, training and experience of the individual, be recognized.

In Civil Justice—That Negroes shall be given equal justice with others in the courts of the land. Ways and means to this end should be supplied by the co-operation of citizens of good will in furnishing legal aid to the indigent and unfortunate.

In Housing—That housing improvement programs that will include Negro residences be inaugurated in all cities, towns and counties, to the end that all our people may dwell in comfortable and adequate houses, and that rental ceilings be controlled by public regulations.

In Religious Leadership—That Christian bodies of both races shall create and maintain co-operatively means for training such religious leaders, both lay and cleric, as can and will develop the best religious life of the Negro race; and particularly that the Baptist bodies of the South co-operate in providing education for Negro ministers equal to that now provided in the seminaries at Louisville, Fort Worth, and New Orleans: Southern Baptist, 1945.

EDUCATION AND ACTION

1. A. The General Council of Congregational Christian Churches endorses the resolution of its Executive Committee taken in open meeting at Cleveland, Ohio, on January 31, 1946, calling for a major emphasis on race relations for the biennium 1946-1948 and the co-ordination of the programs of the several Boards and agencies toward that end.
   B. This biennial program of emphasis is to be concerned with relationships between all ethnic, religious, national, and cultural groups, combating not only the sins of racial and national pride but also of religious bigotry.
   C. The Executive Committee of the General Council is authorized to establish a widely representative committee of lay people and ministers and to select its membership, which committee shall forward this program of emphasis.
   D. The Missions Board and other national agencies of the denomination, the State Conferences, the Association, and the local churches are urged to co-operate fully in this emphasis, using all the resources at our command to reach the conscience of each member of our fellowship: Congregational Christian, 1946.

2. Commend the Department of Social Education and Action of the Board of Christian Education for undertaking the study of racial and cultural relations and direct the Department to report to next General Assembly recommendations whereby the Presbyterian Church may effectively work for a non-segregated church and a non-segregated society: Presbyterian U.S.A., 1946.

3. Direct the Division of Social Education and Action of the Board of Christian Education to disseminate information whereby the individual church of our denomination may work more effectively to eliminate discrimination in all its forms: Presbyterian U.S.A., 1947.

4. Designate the years 1948-1949 for a special emphasis on race relations and call upon all agencies, congregations, judicatories, and members of the Church to examine their own policies and practices and to take appropriate action: Evangelical and Reformed, 1947.

5. In most communities we believe that the establishment by all the churches of interracial committees . . . would be exceedingly

helpful: Presbyterian U.S., 1945.

6. Opportunities for worship in which members of both races will participate should also be arranged as a means to greater sympathy and understanding whenever this is possible: Presbyterian U.S., 1945.

7. The Church, through its pulpit and through its various organizations, should constantly seek to emphasize the necessity for bringing Christian principles into practice in the matter of race relations. It is highly important that contact be maintained between Christians of both races and that these should consult and co-operate with one another in the reduction of racial friction and the encouragement of mutual understanding and helpfulness: Presbyterian U.S., 1945.

8. Recommend that local congregations and districts acquaint themselves with the race difficulties in their areas and undertake projects of friendly helpfulness of any racial groups in need: Brethren, 1945.

9. Call for a greater emphasis on Christian education throughout our brotherhood: Brethren, 1946.

10. Suggest that church groups be organized to study the historical and cultural background of other races with a view to sympathetic understanding and co-operation: Reformed Church in America, 1945.

11. We recommend, in the light of the relation of Southern Baptists to the racial problems of our land, and in the light of our brotherly relationship with three and a half million Negro Baptists in the South, that the Convention appoint a committee . . . to review the service now being rendered by Southern Baptists to the Negro race, to study the whole race situation, especially in its moral and religious aspects and meaning, to consider the responsibility of Baptists in the problems of adjustments of interracial relations, and make recommendations of procedure to the Convention, looking toward a larger fulfillment of our responsibility in the total situation and particularly with reference to helpful co-operation with our fellow Baptists in the Negro race: Southern Baptists, 1946.

12. We shall think of the Negro as a person and treat him accordingly.

    We shall continually strive as individuals to conquer all prejudice and eliminate from our speech terms of contempt and from our conduct actions of ill-will.

We shall teach our children that prejudice is un-Christian and that good will and helpful deeds are the duty of every Christian toward all men of all races.

We shall protest against injustice and indignities against Negroes, as we do in the case of people of our own race, whenever and wherever we meet them.

We shall be willing for the Negro to enjoy the rights granted to him under the Constitution of the United States, including the right to vote, to serve on juries, to receive justice in court, to be free from mob violence, to secure a just share of the benefits of educational and other funds, and to receive equal service for equal payment on public carriers and conveniences.

We shall be just in our dealing with the Negro as an individual. Whenever he is in our employ we shall pay him an adequate wage and provide for him healthful working conditions.

We shall strive to promote community good will between the races in every way possible.

We shall actively co-operate with Negro Baptists in the building of their churches, the education of their ministers, and the promotion of their missions and evangelistic programs.

Your committee, in accordance with the instruction of the Convention, makes the following recommendation:

a. That the Convention recognize its responsibility for the promotion of interracial good will, and urge upon our Baptist people and all Christians the duty of ordering our racial attitudes and actions in accordance with Christian truth and Christian love.

b. That the Convention express its approval of co-operative service, much as is being carried on by the Home Mission Board, the American Baptist Theological Seminary and the Convention Seminaries, in the field of Negro religious and theological education, and by the Woman's Union in its program of education and missionary co-operation.

c. That the Convention approve a long-range program of education among our own people looking toward racial understanding and Christian attitudes in the solution of race problems, and encourage Baptist agencies and institutions to promote such a program, including such particular services as the following: (1) the practice of the Sunday School Board of dealing with the race question in its literature; (2) the publication and distributions of tracts, study course books and other literature dealing with Christianity and race; (3) the publication of editorials, and contributed articles on race relations in denominational papers; (4) the inclusion of the subject of race relations in the social service reports of all state conventions and district associations; (6) (sic) the introduction of courses in race, race relations and Negro life in the curricula of our Baptist colleges; (7) the publication from time to time of summaries of the work of Baptists in this field of service; (8) the co-operation of pastors in bringing to the attention of their people the basic Christian doctrines and principles of conduct that bear upon racial attitudes.

d. That the Convention assign to the Social Service Commission particularly the task of fostering such a program of education and promoting such practical services as the following: (1) supplying pastors with practical suggestions concerning ways in which they can help Negro pastors; (2) encouraging definite work by churches in behalf of the Negro Baptist people of their communities; (3) encouraging discussion of race relations under wise leadership in pastors conferences, district associations, student conferences and brotherhood meetings, and furnishing constructive material for such discussions; (4) seeking the establishment of Departments of Interracial Co-operation by State Conventions (of the order of that in Texas); (5) counseling with Negro Baptist leaders annually concerning the common interests and tasks of white and Negro Baptists in the service of the Kingdom of God; (7) (sic) keeping informed about the work of other organizations in this field.

e. That the Convention assign to the Public Relations Committee the task of keeping informed concerning legislation and other governmental actions touching race relations, human rights and citizenship rights of minority groups; and also of expressing the Baptist principles of democratic freedom and justice in situations that call for their emphasis.

f. That the Convention recognize the value of the interconvention Committee on Negro Ministerial Education and continue it as a standing committee of the Convention.

Southern Baptists, 1947 (from *Book of Reports*).

GENERAL

1. Call attention to desperate need for improving status of non-white peoples in sections of Africa and Asia, keeping in mind that the pattern of race relationships in our own country has profound influence abroad: Northern Baptist, 1946.

2. Christians should not hesitate to support the equality of all races in justice and in law and in access to educational, employment, health, and cultural opportunities: Presbyterian U.S.A., 1945.

3. Lay upon the consciences of all Presbyterians the duty of having their personal attitudes transformed by their devotion to Christ, and the further duty of initiating adventures in interracial understanding and of engaging in every individual and group activity that will bring them and their communities nearer to the Christian ideal of brotherhood. Notable examples of this are the city-wide interracial fellowships; the Interracial Church in San Francisco, supported in part by the presbytery of San Francisco; the Springfield Plan of Cultural Education; and the Sydenham Hospital Plan of New York City: Presbyterian U.S.A., 1945.

4. Encourage friendly approaches between races and between Churches materially to lessen segregation and discrimination: Presbyterian U.S.A., 1946.

5. Recommend that our American Board of Missions seek to expand its work among the colored race through the establishment of Churches, in the rapidly growing Negro communities of the North: United Presbyterian, 1945.

6. We recommend that we stand against race segregation as undemocratic and un-Christian, that we participate in interracial activities in our location, and that we align ourselves on the side of justice and equality in every local situation where racial tension or trouble may arise: United Presbyterian, 1946.

7. We know that there are discriminations against Negroes because they are Negroes in matters such as freedom to vote, economic employment and remuneration, education, housing, military and government service, treatment in courts of justice, and public privileges: Southern Baptist, 1946.

8. Urge upon our people the practice of the principles of Christian brotherhood in dealing with peoples of other races, color, and nationalities: United Lutheran Church in America, 1946.

9. Recommend the observance of Race Relations Sunday: Reformed Church in America, 1945.

10. We call upon every church to study the growing experience of those congregations that have opened their membership to all who live in the community with no barrier on account of race or national origin. Recommend that the problem of race is of such a nature that it behooves the church to study it from every

possible angle, with the view of finding ultimate solutions for various aspects of the problem: Reformed Church in America, 1946.

11. General Synod encourages pastors of congregations which do not otherwise have interracial associations to avail themselves of the opportunity to be active in interracial projects within the community. Such projects afford an opportunity for pastors to work with members of other races and to enlist the intelligent and sympathetic response of layman to the principle of integration: Evangelical and Reformed, 1947.

12. Encourage members of congregations to feel their responsibility for overcoming discriminatory social and economic customs and practices, and co-operate for the combating of restrictive housing covenants, unequal opportunities for education, employment, recreation, housing, and legal protection: Evangelical and Reformed, 1947.

REPORT OF PRESIDENT'S COMMITTEE ON CIVIL RIGHTS

1. Commend the statement to all church people, as a document worthy of study: Federal Council of Churches, 1947.

Appendix II

NEGRO PARTICIPATION IN PREDOMINANTLY WHITE CHURCHES[1]

A. CONGREGATIONAL CHRISTIAN CHURCHES

	NUMBER OF CHURCHES	NEGRO ATTENDANTS	NEGRO MEMBERS
California	6	115	111
Colorado	1	1	0
Connecticut	20	60	40
Illinois	3	4	1
Iowa	2	5	4
Maine	2	9	0
Massachusetts	19	150	159
Michigan	2	11	1
Minnesota	1	1	1
New Hampshire	1	2	0
New Jersey	1	0	2
New York	5	11	8
Ohio	3	8	3
Pennsylvania	1	1	1
Rhode Island	3	12	0
South Dakota	1	2	2
Vermont	3	4	1
Wisconsin	1	3	3

B. NORTHERN BAPTIST CONVENTION

	NUMBER OF CHURCHES	NEGRO ATTENDANTS	NEGRO MEMBERS
California	2	4	1
Connecticut	5	8	3

[1] For methods by which this information was obtained, see footnote 1, page 65, and Table 11, page 67. The total number of churches in the tables is less than the number given in Table II and the related text because churches whose Negro participation consists only of children in Sunday School or Daily Vacation Bible School or adults who attend very rarely have been omitted.

For these reasons there is no table showing Negro participation in Evangelical and Reformed Churches.

B. NORTHERN BAPTIST CONVENTION (Continued)

	NUMBER OF CHURCHES	NEGRO ATTENDANTS	NEGRO MEMBERS
Idaho	1	2	0
Illinois	8	18	9
Indiana	1	2	3
Iowa	2	2	0
Kansas	1	2	5
Maine	3	10	2
Massachusetts	7	55	61
Michigan	6	15	9
Minnesota	1	4	4
New Hampshire	1	2	0
New Jersey	3	6	4
New York	14	30	31
Ohio	5	18	6
Pennsylvania	8	37	4
Rhode Island	2	4	1
South Dakota	1	1	0
Vermont	2	3	0
Washington	1	3	4
West Virginia	2	2	2
Wisconsin	3	6	0

C. UNITED PRESBYTERIAN CHURCH

	NUMBER OF CHURCHES	NEGRO ATTENDANTS	NEGRO MEMBERS
California	1	10	0
Kansas	2	5	0
New York	1	0	4
Ohio	1	1	1
Pennsylvania	4	3	10

D. CHURCH OF THE BRETHREN

	NUMBER OF CHURCHES	NEGRO ATTENDANTS	NEGRO MEMBERS
California	1	5	0
Illinois	1	2	3

E. Protestant Episcopal Church

	NUMBER OF CHURCHES	NEGRO ATTENDANTS	NEGRO MEMBERS
California	8	15	27
Connecticut	4	8	7
Delaware	1	1	1
Iowa	2	2	1
Kansas	2	3	2
Kentucky	1	1	1
Louisiana	1	1	1
Maine	3	12	36
Massachusetts	22	240	282
Michigan	4	6	37
Minnesota	2	2	12
Missouri	1	2	1
Montana	2	4	2
New Jersey	7	32	20
New York	21	100	303
Ohio	5	17	28
Oklahoma	1	1	1
Pennsylvania	7	21	41
Utah	1	2	2
Virginia	1	0	1
Washington	1	0	10

Appendix III

NEGRO ENROLLMENT IN DENOMINATIONAL EDUCATIONAL INSTITUTIONS

A. Negro Enrollment in Church-Controlled Northern Colleges[1]

INSTITUTION	NEGROES ADMITTED 1939-44	1944-45	AVERAGE CIVILIAN ENROLLMENT 1939-44	1944-45	TYPE[2]	CHURCH
CALIFORNIA						
LaVerne Coll............	1	0	175	100	C	Chr. Breth.
Univ. of Redlands.......	No reply		...	785[3]	C	N. Bapt.
COLORADO						
Univ. of Denver.........	No reply		...	2799[3]	C	Meth.
IDAHO						
Coll. of Idaho..........	0	0	450	199	C	Pres. U.S.A.
ILLINOIS						
Carthage Coll..........	1	1	250	180	C	Un. Luth.
Elmhurst Coll..........	0	0	361	229	C	Evan. & Ref.
Illinois Wesleyan Univ...	?	3	750	420	C	Meth.
James Millikin Univ.....	6	1	?	275[3]	C	Pres. U.S.A.
Lake Forest Coll........	No reply		...	232[3]	C	Pres. U.S.A.
MacMurray Coll. for Women..............	0	0	628	712	W	Meth.
McKendree Coll........	No reply		...	88[3]	C	Meth.
Monmouth Coll........	0	0	500	279	C	Un. Pres.
North Central Coll......	0	0	525	410	C	Evan.
Shurtleff Coll...........	No reply		...	492[3]	C	N. Bapt.
INDIANA						
Butler Univ.............	No reply		...	1584[3]	C	Disc.
DePauw Univ...........	0	1	1500	1210	C	Meth.
Earlham Coll............	11	6	...	340[3]	C	Friends 5-Yr. Mtg.
Franklin Coll...........	?	7	300	225	C	N. Bapt.
Hanover Coll...........	0	0	?	170	C	Pres. U.S.A.
Indiana Central Coll.....	15	9	302	144	C	Un. Breth.
Manchester Coll........	?	2	401	415	C	Ch. Breth.
IOWA						
Buena Vista Coll........	0	0	300	200	C	Pres. U.S.A.
Central Coll............	0	2	350	215	C	Ref. Am.
Cornell Coll............	0	0	?	531	C	Meth.
Iowa Wesleyan Coll.....	1	1	400	165	C	Meth.
Morningside Coll.......	No reply		...	375[3]	C	Meth.
Parsons Coll...........	1	0	380	141	C	Pres. U.S.A.
Simpson Coll...........	No reply		...	269[3]	C	Meth.
Univ. of Dubuque.......	?	?	?	530[3]	C	Pres. U.S.A.
Western Union Coll......	0	0	430	250	C	Evan.
William Penn Coll.......	7	1	...	185[3]	C	Friends 5-Yr. Mtg.

[1] Church-controlled according to *Educational Directory, 1944-45.*

[2] C—Co-educational; M—Men only; W—Women only.

[3] These figures from *1945 World Almanac,* are based on "Questionnaires returned in 1944." All other figures are taken from postcard replies.

INSTITUTION	NEGROES ADMITTED		AVERAGE CIVILIAN ENROLLMENT		TYPE[2]	CHURCH
	1939-44	1944-45	1939-44	1944-45		
KANSAS						
Baker Univ............	2	0	381	248	C	Meth.
Coll. of Emporia........	0	0	325	140	C	Pres. U.S.A.
Friends Univ............	30	8	...	263[3]	C	Friends
Kansas Wesleyan Univ...	0	0	400	426	C	Meth.
McPherson Coll.........	0	0	350	165	C	Ch. Breth.
Ottawa Univ............	3	0	300	170	C	N. Bapt.
Southwestern Coll......	4	2	500	322	C	Meth.
Sterling Coll...........	13	0	227	137	C	Un. Pres.
MICHIGAN						
Adrian Coll............	?	3	180	162	C	Meth.
Albion Coll............	1	1	700	594	C	Meth.
Alma Coll.............	No reply		...	478[3]	C	Pres. U.S.A.
Hope Coll.............	?	0	575	325	C	Ref. Am.
Kalamazoo Coll........	0	0	405	266	C	N. Bapt.
MINNESOTA						
Hamline Univ..........	No reply		...	533[3]	C	Meth.
NEBRASKA						
Doane Coll............	0	0	?	130	C	Cong. Chr.
Hastings Coll..........	3	0	500	250	C	Pres. U.S.A.
Midland Coll...........	1	0	325	175	C	U. Luth.
Nebraska Central Coll. ..	0	0	75	70	C	Friends 5-Yr. Mtg.
Nebraska Wesleyan Univ.	5	0	400	300	C	Meth.
York Coll.............	0	0	215	119	C	Un. Breth.
NEW JERSEY						
Bloomfield Coll. & Sem...	4	2	100	75	C	Pres. U.S.A.
Drew Univ............	No reply		...	563[3]	M (Sem. Co-ed.)	Meth.
NEW YORK						
Hartwick Coll..........	0	0	300	130	C	Un. Luth.
Keuka Coll............	No reply		...	288[3]	W	N. Bapt.
Wagner Memorial Lutheran Coll............	7	1	250	275	C	Un. Luth.
NORTH DAKOTA						
Jamestown Coll........	0	0	475	253	C	Pres. U.S.A.
OHIO						
Baldwin-Wallace Coll....	?	4	700	450	C	Meth.
Coll. of Wooster........	?	1	842	650	C	Pres. U.S.A.
Defiance Coll...........	No reply		...	210[3]	C	Cong. Chr.
Denison Univ...........	1	1	821	675	C	N. Bapt.
Heidelberg Coll.........	2	3	300	153	M	Evan. & Ref.
Mount Union Coll.......	8	2	600	400	C	Meth.
Muskingum Coll........	2	1	600	495	C	Un. Pres.
Ohio Northern Univ.....	No reply		...	300[3]	C	Meth.
Ohio Wesleyan Univ.....	No reply		...	1448[3]	C	Meth.
Otterbein Coll..........	0	0	?	400	C	Un. Breth.
Wilmington Coll........	3	1	300	190	C	Friends 5-Yr. Mtg.
Wittenberg Coll........	20	9	604	413	C	Un. Luth.

[2] C—Co-educational; M—Men only; W—Women only.
[3] These figures from *1945 World Almanac*, are based on "Questionnaires returned in 1944." All other figures are taken from postcard replies.

INSTITUTION	NEGROES ADMITTED		AVERAGE CIVILIAN ENROLLMENT		TYPE[2]	CHURCH
	1939-44	1944-45	1939-44	1944-45		
OREGON						
Lewis & Clark Coll......	2	1	180	130	C	Pres. U.S.A.
Linfield Coll.............	No reply		...	247[3]	C	N. Bapt.
Pacific Coll.............	0	?	100	100	C	Friends
Williamette Coll.........	3	1	700	650	C	Meth.
PENNSYLVANIA						
Albright Coll............	0	0	?	232[3]	C	Evan.
Beaver Coll.............	No reply		...	600[3]	W	Pres. U.S.A.
Bucknell Univ...........	0	1	1300	1000	C	N. Bapt.
Cedar Crest Coll.........	No reply		...	330[3]	W	Evan. & Ref.
Elizabethtown Coll......	2	?	250	250	C	Ch. Breth.
Franklin & Marshall Coll.	0	0	600	500	M	Evan. & Ref.
Gettysburg Coll.........	No reply		...	332[3]	C	Un. Luth.
Haverford Coll.........	1	1	...	350[3]	M	Friends
Juniata Coll.............	No reply		...	249[3]	C	Ch. Breth.
Lafayette Coll..........	No reply		...	1500[3]	M	Pres. U.S.A.
Lebanon Valley Coll.....	0	0	200	200	C	Un. Breth.
Muhlenberg Coll.........	0	0	500	390	M	Un. Luth.
Susquehanna Univ.......	0	0	250	258	C	Un. Luth.
Swarthmore Coll.........	2	4	...	691[3]	C	Friends
Thiel Coll...............	No reply		...	115[3]	C	Un. Luth.
Waynesburg Coll.........	2	0	251	149	M	Pres. U.S.A.
Westminster Coll........	1	?	690	453	C	Un. Pres.
Wilson Coll.............	No reply		...	400[3]	W	Pres. U.S.A.
SOUTH DAKOTA						
Dakota Wesleyan Univ...	No reply		...	158[3]	C	Meth.
Huron Coll.............	No reply		...	107[3]	C	Pres. U.S.A.
WASHINGTON						
Coll. of Puget Sound.....	No reply		...	520[3]	C	Meth.
Whitworth Coll..........	No reply		...	514[3]	C	Pres. U.S.A.
WISCONSIN						
Carroll Coll.............	0	0	550	230	C	Pres. U.S.A.
Mission House Coll. and Theo. Sem.............	0	0	184	96	C	Evan. & Ref.
Northland Coll..........	No reply		...	108[3]	C	Cong. Chr.

[2] C—Co-educational; M—Men only; W—Women only.
[3] These figures from *1945 World Almanac,* are based on "Questionnaires returned in 1944." All other figures are taken from postcard replies.

B. Negro Enrollment in Church-Controlled Colleges in Border Areas

Information was sought from fifteen church-controlled colleges in the states of Maryland, Missouri, W. Virginia, and the District of Columbia. Only two of these reported Negro students: Alderson Broaddus College in W. Virginia, one in 1939-1944 and one in 1944-945; and American University, District of Columbia, 109 in 1944-1945.

C. NEGRO ENROLLMENT IN CHURCH-CONTROLLED JUNIOR COLLEGES

Information was sought from sixteen church-controlled junior colleges. Only two reported Negro students: Evanston Collegiate Institute, Illinois, seven for the five-year period 1939-1944 and three for 1944-1945; Northwestern Junior College, Iowa, two for the five-year period 1939-1944.

D. NEGRO ENROLLMENT IN CHURCH-RELATED ELEMENTARY AND SECONDARY SCHOOLS

Information was sought from church-controlled preparatory schools. Only two reported Negro students: the Oakwood School (Friends), Poughkeepsie, New York, six for the five-year period 1939-1944, four for 1944-1945; the Pacific-Ackworth School (Friends), Arcadia, California, one in the five-year period 1939-1944; Media Friends' School, Media, Pennsylvania, one in 1944-1945.

E. NEGRO ENROLLMENT IN CHURCH-CONTROLLED NORTHERN THEOLOGICAL SEMINARIES[1]

INSTITUTION	NEGROES ADMITTED		AVERAGE CIVILIAN ENROLLMENT		TYPE[2]	CHURCH
	1939-44	1944-45	1939-44	1944-45		
CALIFORNIA						
Berkeley Baptist Div. Sch.	6	7	145	169	C	N. Bapt.
Church Div. Sch. of Pacific	0	0	24	18	M	P. E.
San Francisco Theo. Sem.	0	1	99	81	C	Pres. U.S.A.
COLORADO						
Iliff School of Theo.......	3	1	123	116	C	Meth.
CONNECTICUT						
Berkley Div. Sch........	0	0	27	11	M	P. E.
ILLINOIS						
Bethany Biblical Sem....	1	0	...	238	C	Ch. Breth.
Chicago Lutheran Theo. Sem.................	2	0	30	`38	M	Luth.
Chicago Theo. Sem......	8	1	120	112	C	Cong. Chr.
Evangelical Theo. Sem...	0	0	80	82	C	Evan.
Garrett Biblical Inst.....	?	3	270	290	C	Meth.
McCormick Theo. Sem...	3	0	...	175	M	Pres. U.S.A.
Seabury-Western........	..	..	...	...	M	P. E.
North Bap. Theo. Sem...	..	..	...	...	C	N. Bapt.
INDIANA						
Sch. of Religion, Butler Univ...............	3	1	110	132	C	Disc.
IOWA						
Theo. Sem., Univ. of Dubuque............	0	0	40	44	C	Pres. U.S.A.
KANSAS						
Central Baptist Theo. Sem.................	3	3	131	204	C	N. Bapt.
MAINE						
Bangor Theo. Sem.......	0	0	...	...	C	Cong. Chr.

[1] Church-controlled according to *Educational Directory, 1944-45*.
[2] C—Co-educational; M—Men only; W—Women only

INSTITUTION	NEGROES ADMITTED		AVERAGE CIVILIAN ENROLLMENT		TYPE[2]	CHURCH
	1939-44	1944-45	1939-44	1944-45		
MASSACHUSETTS						
Episcopal Theo. Sem.....	0	0	...	...	C	P. E.
Andover Newton Theo. Sem.................	..	..	...	...	C	N. Bapt. Cong. Chr.
MICHIGAN						
Western Theo. Sem......	0	0	51	45	M	Ref. Am.
MINNESOTA						
Bethel Institute.........	1	1	200	220	C	N. Bapt.
N. W. Luth. Theo. Sem...	0	0	28	38	M	Un. Luth.
NEBRASKA						
Western Theo. Sem. (Theo. Sch. of Midland Coll.).	0	0	...	18	M	Un. Luth.
NEW JERSEY						
Drew Theo. Sem. (Part of Drew University).....	..	..	...	...	C	Meth.
New Brunswick Theo. Sem.................	1	0	...	30	M	Ref. Am.
Princeton Theo. Sem.....	..	..	...	...	M	Pres. U.S.A.
NEW YORK						
Colgate-Rochester Div. Sch.................	9	2	116	99	C	N. Bapt.
General Theo. Sem.......	9	4	100	64	C	P. E.
OHIO						
Bonebrake Theo. Sem....	1	0	110	121	C	Un. Breth.
PENNSYLVANIA						
Crozer Sem............	11	6	70	60	C	N. Bapt.
Eastern Baptist Theo. Sem.................	?	?	275	...	C	N. Bapt.
Evangelical Sch. of Theo.	1	0	30	30	C	Evan.
Theo. Sem. of the Evan. & Reformed Church.....	0	0	58	61	M	Evan. & Ref.
Lutheran Theo. Sem. Phila.................	0	0	80	90	M	Un. Luth.
Divinity Sch. of the P. E. Church.............	1	3	20	15	M	P. E.
Pittsburgh-Xenia Theo. Sem.................	7	?	60	38	M	Un. Pres.
Western Theo. Sem......	8	5	90	79	M	Pres. U.S.A.
Lutheran Theo. Sem., Gettysburg...........	No reply		...	...	M	Un. Luth.
WISCONSIN						
Nashotah House (Theo. Sem.)................	No reply		...	...	M	P. E.

F. Negro Enrollment in Church-Controlled Theological Seminaries in Border Areas

INSTITUTION	NEGROES ADMITTED		AVERAGE CIVILIAN ENROLLMENT		TYPE	CHURCH
MARYLAND						
Westminster Theo. Sem..	No reply		...	...	C	Meth.
MISSOURI						
Eden Theo. Sem.........	0	0	70	75	C	Evan. & Ref.

[2] C—Co-educational; M—Men only; W—Women only.

Index